Cooking with The Clover Mill

Delicious Ayurvedic Recipes

Julie Dent

Contents

Introduction ... 1

What is Ayurveda? ... 3

- What is my dosha? ... 3
- Vata – space and air ... 5
- Pitta – fire and water ... 6
- Kapha – water and earth ... 7

What does Ayurveda mean to me? ... 9

How to eat according to Ayurvedic principles ... 13

RECIPES

- Ghee ... 17

Breakfasts

- The Clover Mill porridge ... 21
- Porridge without oats! ... 22
- Golden rice porridge ... 23
- Fermented mung bean pancakes ... 24
- Coconut pancakes ... 27
- Stewed fruits ... 28
- Gut-protecting apple porridge ... 29
- Overnight muesli ... 31
- Toasted oats muesli) ... 32
- Bubble and squeak eggs ... 33

Soups

- Basic stock recipe ... 37
- Pea and mint soup ... 39
- Wild garlic soup – with or without nettles ... 41
- Carrot and ginger soup ... 43

Roasted leek and fennel soup .45
Beetroot and apple soup .47
Mung bean soup .48
Welcome soup .49
Red lentil and chard soup .51
Sweet Potato and Rosemary Soup .52
Parsnip and apple soup .53
Broccoli and sunflower seed soup .55
Soup garnishes .56
Pesto .57

Pâté and dips

Carrot and Cumin Pâté .61
Beetroot and Walnut Pâté .63
Hummus .64
Sunflower Seed Pâté .66
Shitake mushroom pâté .67
Herby Yoghurt Dip .69
Pumpkin Seed Pâté .71
Raita .72

Savoury snacks, breads and crackers

Seed crackers .75
Sri Lankan rotis .77
Mung bean and wild garlic bread .79
Superseed bread .81
Savoury muffins .82

Main and side dishes

Kitcheri or kitchadi .86
Superseed tart .89
Lentil-stuffed chard leaves .91
Korma curry .92
Pumpkin or squash curry .95
Beetroot curry .96
Courgette and dill fritters .97
Sweet potato and mung bean curry .99

Beetroot burgers ... 101
Beetroot risotto ... 102
Cabbage subji ... 103
Stuffed butternut squash ... 105
Asparagus soufflés ... 107
Roasted vegetable quinoa ... 108
Cauliflower or broccoli rice ... 109
Vegetable mash – potato alternatives ... 110
Roasted vegetables ... 111

Sauces and chutneys

Apple and ginger chutney ... 115
Avocado sauce ... 116
Tahini sauce ... 116
Courgette sauce ... 117
Tarragon dressing ... 117
Cherry and orange chutney ... 118
Damson chutney ... 119
Fresh ginger chutney ... 121

Desserts

Baked spiced apples ... 125
Poached pears ... 126
Ginger cream ... 126
Biscotti ... 127
Chia coconut pudding ... 128
Gogi dessert ... 129
Raw chocolate mousse torte ... 130
Fragrant rice pudding ... 132
Gluten-free fruit crumble ... 133
Baobab and lemon mousse cake ... 135
Coconut panna cotta with fruit coulis ... 137
Mango surprise ... 138

Cakes, bars and biscuits

Ginger cake ... 141
Date and prune cake ... 143

Damson or apple cake . . . 145
Vegan chocolate brownies . . . 147
Apple flapjacks . . . 148
Plump-a-balls . . . 149
Pom bombs . . . 150
Bliss balls or modak . . . 152
Digest-a-balls . . . 155
Chocolate beetroot cake . . . 156

Teas

The Clover Mill chai . . . 159
Spice teas . . . 161
The Clover Mill morning tea . . . 162

Cordials

Elderflower cordial . . . 165
Elderberry cordial . . . 166

Milks

Golden milk . . . 168
Nut milk . . . 169
Matcha latte . . . 170
Hemp hot chocolate . . . 171

Food cupboard essentials and nice-to-have . . . 173
Resources . . . 175
Bibliography and recommended reading . . . 177

Cooking
WITH
The
CLOVER
Mill

Introduction

This book has been written in response to all the requests, demands even(!) for The Clover Mill recipes. I've spent the last seven years developing our Ayurveda and Yoga Retreats here and cooking Ayurveda-inspired meals for our wonderful guests. This book includes over one hundred of the most common recipes served during the year.

A huge heartfelt thank you to all our thoughtful guests who have given me positive feedback and encouragement over the years, to all the authors of the zillions of cookbooks, blogs and Instagram posts I've indulged in, and wonderful kind friends who've encouraged me all the way.

This book certainly isn't designed to be a comprehensive introduction to Ayurveda; there are many out there already. Ayurveda cookbooks usually designate each recipe as being suitable for the different *dosha* types. I've occasionally done this, but most of the recipes in this book are suitable for all types and I'd like to invite you to learn more about your doshas (see later pages and resources at end of this book) and to listen to your own bodies after each meal and see how foods make you feel. Even if you eat something that isn't really great for your type, providing you don't eat it day in, day out, then it really won't do you too much harm. Think variety rather than worrying too much about every ingredient. Keep meals simple, they don't need to have twenty-five ingredients, and try to stick to the guidelines for ayurvedic cooking found later in the book. If you cook from scratch, use fresh ingredients, include plenty of seasonal vegetables and add a few herbs and spices then you will be 90 per cent there. Oh, and try to make only as much as you need to eat that day as leftovers have less *prana* (energy) and vitality.

Most recipes in this book serve four people, and most can be halved for two or doubled for eight, but if you are serving larger numbers, you will probably have to reduce the amount of liquid. It's one of the weird rules of chemistry! Some of my recipes use cups and some grammes, this is just the way I altered and developed them over the years. A set of measuring cups are cheap and will save you a lot of time weighing. And unless you are making a cake, then you don't need to be so accurate, relax and have a go.

We serve a slightly different menu on the special Rest & Digest Retreats where we teach and show guests how to reduce the amount of time we spend in fight/flight mode and increase the time our rest and digest parasympathetic nervous system is active. Alongside the special yoga, massages, breathwork and meditation, we serve meals designed to reduce *vata* and to decrease the harmful, and increase the beneficial, bacteria in our gut microbiome. This is particularly close to my heart as my first fascinating and rewarding career was diagnostic microbiology. These recipes to improve our gut microbiome will be detailed in a separate book.

Please enjoy learning more about your mind and body, enjoy cooking and eating these recipes, have fun with them, and be healthy and happy.

What is Ayurveda?

The word *Ayurveda* comprises *ayur* which means life, and *veda* which means science or knowledge, so Ayurveda means the science or knowledge of life, how to live a healthy life, how to live wisely. More than a comprehensive medical system, Ayurveda is a detailed lifestyle with emphasis on assuming personal responsibility for our values and actions towards achieving perfect health in mind, body and spirit. The theory and practices of Ayurveda have developed, and been tried and tested, over thousands of years and importantly are absolutely relevant to today.

What is my dosha?

There are many great books out there that give a comprehensive explanation – here are a few key facts which hopefully will inspire you to learn more.

Everything and every person is made up of the five fundamental principles or elements of space (ether), air, fire, water and earth. The predominance of each element changes continuously, modifying temperature, humidity, time and seasons. The proportions of these five elements vary from person to person and day to day. Keeping your unique proportions the same, throughout life, results in perfect health, but when your ratio is upset, disease may occur. For example, increased earth may lead to weight gain, increased fire may lead to indigestion or stomach ulcers and increased air can lead to fear and anxiety. The five elements combine to form three energies known as *doshas* that control different functions of the body – *vata*, *pitta* and *kapha*. This concept is similar to the concept of the four humours of blood, phlegm, black bile and yellow bile way back around 400 BCE. Hippocrates and Galen associated the humours with the fundamental elements of air, water, earth and fire and also linked them to the seasons. Diet, sleep, exercise and work were seen as key to maintaining health and patients were studied holistically – unfortunately this way of thinking went out of fashion when surgery and dissection took investigation of illness in a different direction in the Western world. But that's enough history for now . . .

In Ayurveda, our unique ratio of vata, pitta and kapha is set at the moment of conception and is known as our *prakruti* and the aim is to maintain our unique constitution throughout life. However, due to our environment, the seasons, relationships, age, diet etc. we can easily go out of balance and our ratio of vata, pitta and kapha no longer is the same as our pakruti and this is known as our *vikruti*. If we remain out of balance for too long, then this will result in mental or physical illness. There are seven possible combinations of vata, pitta and kapha, you may have a dominant dosha or may be a combination of two such as *vata-pitta* or *pitta-kapha*, etc.

We always aim to reduce the predominant dosha of our vikruti as this will be the one causing our symptoms. But first we ask – 'Why isn't my body healing itself?' Our bodies have an amazing capacity to heal, but often need help from ourselves in terms of the right diet and lifestyle to support our unique constitutions. Understanding our pakruti and vikruti enables us to understand our true nature and gives us the tools to keep ourselves in balance.

We are all different. We are all unique.

The characteristics of each dosha type and tips on how to stay in balance can be found in the next few pages.

Vata – space and air

In balance	Out of balance
Great ideas, enthusiastic, energetic, spontaneous. Move, walk and talk quickly. Creative, artistic. Loving, sensitive, imaginative, perceptive, intuitive. Jack of all trades, multi-tasker.	Thinking too much, fear, anxiety, nervousness. Spacey, ungrounded. Emotionally delicate, shy and introverted. Indecisive, tendency to procrastinate, disorganised, poor planners. Difficulty listening and tendency to interrupt others. Talk fast and breathlessly. Arthritis, cracking joints, insomnia, tiredness, constipation, bloating, headaches, food intolerances.

Qualities: dry, light, cold, rough, subtle, mobile, clear.

How to keep in balance:

Lifestyle	Food
Live with natures rhythms, regular meals, regular sleep and waking times. Reduce sensory stimulation especially loud noise, talking too much. Don't suppress natural urges such as eating, urination, defecation, passing wind or resting when tired. Listen to calming music. Meditate. Do gentle exercise such as yoga, tai chi, walking, swimming. Massage whole body daily with warm oil such as sesame and essential oils. Keep warm with baths and showers. Sunbathe. Enjoy fresh flowers.	Mindful eating. Favour sweet, sour, salty tastes. Reduce bitter, astringent, pungent tastes. No coffee, tea, alcohol. Enjoy liquid broths and stews rather than dry foods. Avoid raw, cold food. Drink warm teas, milks with spices to avoid constipation. Sweet juicy soft fruit. Fresh ginger and warming spices such as cumin, cardamom, fennel and coriander.

Pitta – fire and water

In balance	Out of balance
Intelligent, understands new concepts quickly. Courageous, determined, ambitious, dedicated. Joyful, emotionally observant, Great planners, organised, list makers. Confident, hard-working.	Intense, manipulative, jealous, arrogant. Angry, hangry if late for a meal, frustrated, critical and judgemental. Perfectionist, workaholic. OCD and addictions. Acne, eczema, inflammation, ulcers. Heartburn, indigestion, eye disorders. Qualities: oily, light, hot, sharp, liquid, mobile.

How to keep in balance:

Lifestyle	Food
Spend time in nature, especially by cool water. Meditation, yoga, rest, non-competitive activities. Listen to calming music. Cool showers and cooling massage oils such as coconut or aloe vera. Avoid artificial stimulants – alcohol, coffee, drugs. Be aware of emotions through journaling, talking to a good friend. Learn to think 'That's good enough'!	Mindful eating, not whilst working! Include foods with sweet, bitter and astringent tastes at every meal. Favour, cool, dry and heavier foods. Reduce salty, sour and pungent foods. Reduce hot spices – chilli, garlic. Drink warm teas with chamomile, cumin, coriander, fennel, rose, hibiscus, mint, lemongrass.

Kapha – water and earth

In balance	Out of balance
Strong, healthy body. Loving, compassionate, sweet, gentle. Loyal, accepting of others. Calm steady mind, excellent memory. Excellent stamina and durability. Slow and graceful. Deep sleep, refreshed on waking. Good listeners, inherent desire to help others.	Lazy, sluggish, tired, unmotivated, unchanging, unable to say no. Long-term depression, introverted, unable to express thoughts and emotions. Unaware of others. Unable to let go of emotions and possessions. Swelling, water retention, weight gain. Indigestion, constipation, dullness Sinus congestion, excess phlegm.

Qualities: heavy, slow, cool, slimy, dense, soft, static, sticky, cloudy, hard, gross

How to keep in balance:

Lifestyle	Food
No daytime sleeping! Regular dynamic exercise. Aerobic walking in nature. Dancing and listening to energising music. Writing. Drinking warm water, not cold. Waking and rising at sunrise or before. Cooking for others. Decluttering. Warm baths. Essential oils. Fresh flowers. Meditation.	Include foods with pungent, bitter and astringent tastes at every meal. Reduce sweet, sour and salty foods. Eat smaller regular meals, no snacking! Warm light soups and broths. Warm herbal teas. Warming spices like cinnamon, cloves, black pepper, cardamom, turmeric, ginger, pippali, fenugreek, cayenne. Citrus fruits, berries. Reduce fats, oils, nuts, heavy processed foods. Leafy greens. No leftovers!

There are three other important concepts of Ayurveda to bear in mind – *agni*, *ama* and *ojas*.

Agni, from the word for *ignite,* means fire, our digestive fire, which is responsible for our appetite, the digestion of our food, metabolism and assimilation of nutrients. If we have good agni we will be able to digest all foods well, extract all the essential nutrients we need to build our amazing bodies, and also produce ojas – the last product of digestion. Ojas gives us our vitality, immunity, longevity and zest for life, so we need to look after our agni in order to produce sufficient ojas.

If agni is compromised, then partially digested or undigested food left in the gut starts to ferment and turns into ama. Ama means toxins and in Ayurveda is understood as the root cause of all disease. When we have ama our tongue is coated in the mornings, we might feel dull and lethargic, maybe have constipation, gas or indigestion. Ama can cause bad breath, affect our taste and cause mental fog or confusion. If left, it can accumulate and travel to joints to cause arthritis and other systemic disease. Ama prevents the production of precious life-sustaining ojas. Therefore, the elimination of mental and physical ama is an essential component of ayurvedic lifestyle and deep cleansing treatments such as *panchakarma*.

What does Ayurveda mean to me?

the art and science of living wisely, in tune with nature, touching the earth lightly, being well, energised, happy and content.

Nature provides us with all the right nutrition at the right time of year and wild animals understand this, in fact man is the only species to become nutritionally deficient. If we think back to how our recent ancestors lived before supermarkets were available, stocked full of foods from all around the world providing the same fruits and vegetables every day of the year. Our ancestors lived off the land, gorging on summer fruits when available, eating sweet root vegetables and grains in the autumn and winter, then moving on to bitter greens like sorrel, nettles, watercress and wild garlic in the spring. Growing some of our own food provides us with seasonal ingredients that help balance our doshas when they need it. For example, as I'm writing this in autumn, the cold dry wind is blowing, the leaves are swirling around as vata energy is present. So, eating sweet and heavy root vegetables and grains is going to pacify our vata, calm our nerves and ground us, reducing any anxiety or inability to focus. Then in early spring when the root vegetables and grains have all gone, we're left with a light diet of bitter greens. At the mill we grow spinach, kale and chard and forage wild garlic, dandelion leaves etc. which survive the winter and provide the fresh vegetables for guests in spring. This helps clear the body of accumulated kapha from the wintertime and encourages us to get outside in the fresh air and lighten the body with exercise and lighter foods. Of course, not everyone has the resources to grow their own food so just try to be aware of what is grown in the country where you live, try farmers markets, read the supermarket labels for country of origin and aim to eat as seasonally as you can. And do choose organic if you have the resources.

At The Clover Mill we respect nature and the environment and strive to have as little detrimental impact as we can. We have a biomass boiler that provides space heating and hot water to all buildings along highly insulated pipework and a sewage treatment system that relies on aerobic bacteria to do the job. Our 50 metre-deep bore hole supplies delicious alkaline (pH 8) water and we recycle our waste as much as we can. We have hens to not only give us rich tasting eggs packed with vitamin K as they are grass-fed, but they love eating any leftovers and devour peelings that we cook for them – quite rightly they won't eat raw food now! We have a satisfying circle of life central to which are the hens:

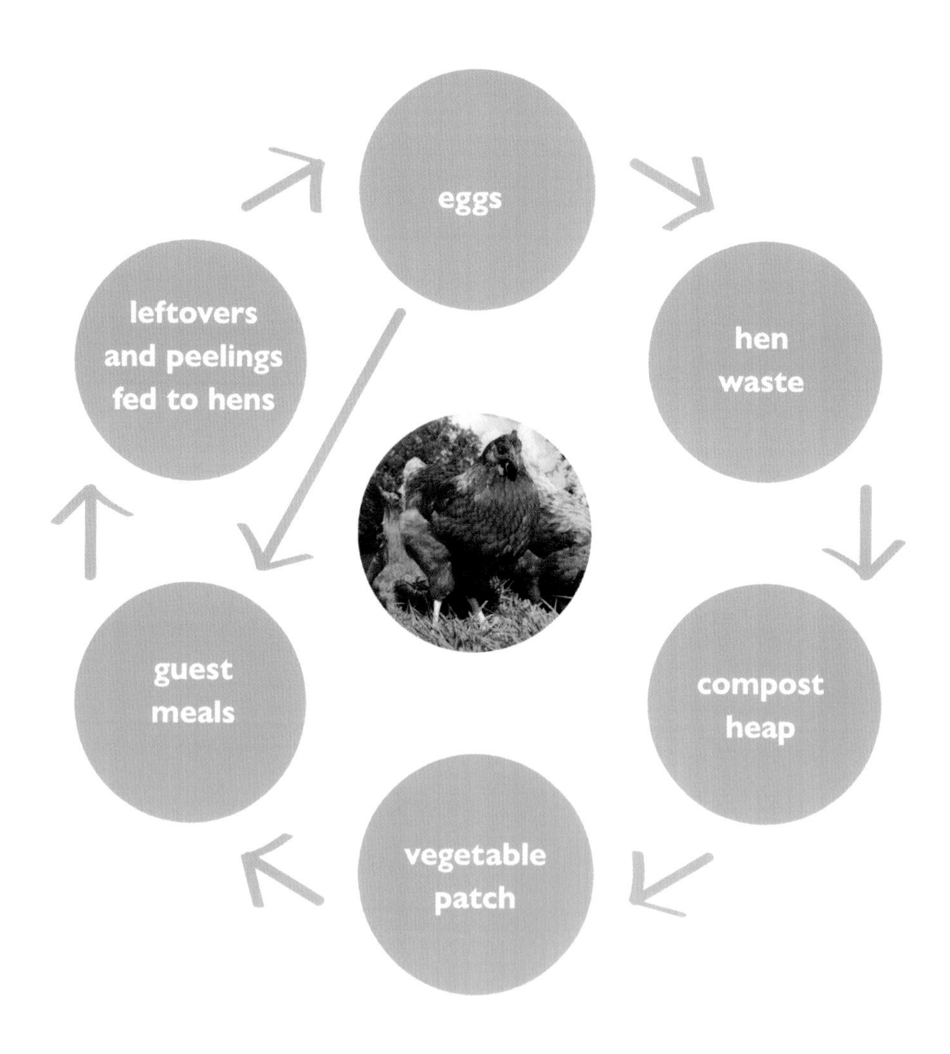

I've always loved to serve friends with plates of colourful food, decorated with flowers or fresh herbs from the garden. Eating the rainbow ensures we have a variety of minerals, phytochemicals, vitamins and antioxidants in our meals. In Ayurveda we also learn that every food has a taste (*rasa*), has a heating or cooling energy (*virya*) and also has a post-digestive effect (*vipaka*). There are six tastes: sweet, sour, salty, astringent, bitter and pungent. Each taste relates to two elements and so each taste affects our doshas. Remember that in Ayurveda like increases like so in order to keep in balance, the majority of our meal should be tastes that are the opposite of our dosha. For example, if we are high vata then if we eat foods that are sweet, sour and salty that will pacify vata as they include earth, water and fire elements. Whereas if you mainly ate bitter, pungent and astringent foods your vata would increase. As always, we need a balance, so add small amounts of the other tastes to satisfy all three doshas; this prevents the craving for something sweet after a meal and then something savoury after dessert.

See diagram below:

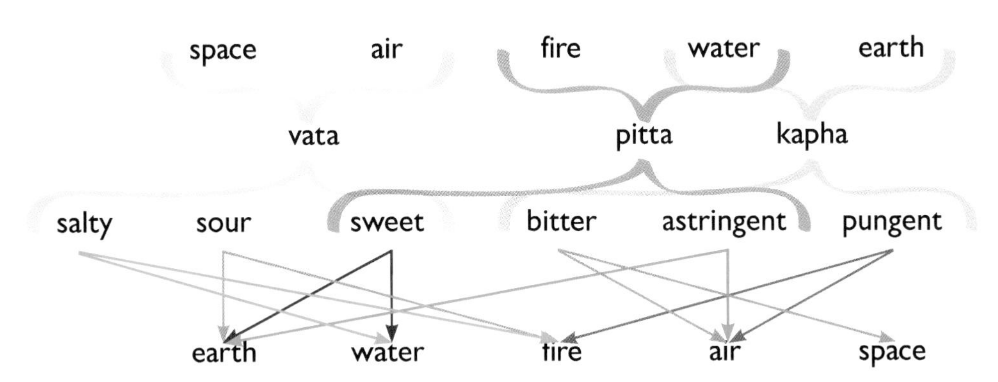

If you've been to one of our retreats you will have learnt a little about the elements, doshas, agni, ama and ojas. These are the fundamentals of Ayurveda which will not only help you to understand yourself and your friends and family, but, more critically, will help you to know what your body needs to eat and when. Instead of annotating every recipe and every ingredient as being suitable for vata, pitta or kapha, I would like to invite you to learn to judge for yourselves.

Also, unless you are going to eat only one dish for the next few months and nothing else, then the odd meal that isn't suitable for you isn't going to cause much harm. If someone with high vata has a large bag of popcorn they might feel a bit more spacey, if a pitta has a huge bowl of hot spicy chilli they might feel a bit hot-headed and if a kapha person eats too much of our amazing baobab mousse cake then they might feel a bit sluggish afterwards. But eating those foods every day, will definitely have a more adverse effect. So, get to know your doshas, get to know yourself, get to know your food and remember variety is key to getting all the tastes and nutrients we need.

eat for your body, mind and doshas

How to eat according to Ayurvedic principles

'What am I going to eat tonight?' is a frequent question guests ask me on the last day of a retreat. So, lets summarise what eating ayurvedically actually means.

Freshly prepare and cook food – nothing processed, no leftovers, not raw.

Add as many spices and culinary herbs as you can – even in tiny amounts that you can't taste – they will still work.

Eat as many vegetables as you can.

Take a moment before eating to focus on the plate in front of you; I like to think 'thank you for the food providers'.

Sip warm water or herbal tea, not cold or iced drinks.

Eat up to two *anjalis** of food with one anjali of liquid at each meal.

Eat mindfully, not in front of the TV, or scanning social media or reading.

Eat peacefully, not when angry or upset.

Eat your biggest meal in pitta time (10 am–2 pm) and eat a light supper (soup) as early as possible.

In addition, when you are ready for the next steps:

Eat according to your dosha.

Eat seasonally.

Avoid certain combinations – 'eat fruit alone or leave fruit alone'; don't combine dairy with meat or fish.

Cook in a clean and tidy kitchen, mindfully and with love!

Put your favourite music on and have some fun preparing food to nourish you and your loved ones.

* cup both your hands together and this gives you your anjali measurement.

One of the simplest and most effective ways to improve digestion and quality of sleep (plus weight loss) is to eat less in the evening and have your biggest meal at lunchtime. This is when the sun and our digestive fire are at their peak – in pitta time 10 am–2 pm. As the sun sets in the evening so does our inner digestive sun (agni). When we eat less in the evening and go to bed by 10 pm with an empty stomach, the body can get to work on eliminating toxins and impurities that have built up during the day, especially on the brain. Without having to digest as we sleep, we are able to repair and rejuvenate ourselves and so wake up with the sun and spring out of bed around 6 am with the lightness of vata, bright, energised and motivated!

eat light at night for good sleep and
great morning energy

Recipes

Notes

....

....

....

....

Ghee

Ghee has to be the first recipe in this book. The Vedas call ghee the 'first and the most essential of all foods' and ghee is a central element of the Vedic culture. Ghee increases intelligence and improves the memory. Ghee increases agni and also ojas, which is the underlying basis of all immunity and the essence of all bodily tissues. Maya Tiwari calls ghee the 'single most ojas-producing food on earth'. In moderation ghee balances all the doshas, can be used to heal burnt or damaged skin, to help herbs penetrate tissues, to treat eyes, is key to panchakarma treatment and is highly nourishing.

Lactose and milk proteins are removed during the process of making ghee making it suitable for those who are lactose intolerant and sometimes I can even persuade vegans to use it! The highest quality ghee is made from milk produced by grass-fed cows, unsalted, unpasteurised and definitely not homogenised. We're lucky to have a local farm with grass-fed cows which produce the creamiest milk ever. It is surprisingly simple (well I was surprised the first time...) to make butter from full-fat milk and then make ghee from the butter.

If you have an hour to spare, it's a peaceful experience, a lovely mindful meditation to produce a beautiful batch of nourishing ghee smelling as sweet as caramel.

Take two or more blocks of butter from grass-fed cows (if possible) and place in a stainless-steel pan on a medium heat. When melted and starting to bubble, reduce the heat to a simmer, still bubbling but as low as you can go. Maya Tiwari likens the sound to rain on a tin roof. The milk solids will form a foam which turns into a white crust on the surface and also sinks to the bottom. Be careful not to burn the deposit on the bottom otherwise the ghee will be dark and bitter. As moisture evaporates off the ghee (clarified butter) will become clear and golden with a wonderful caramel smell. And when it stops raining, then it's ready.

Leave to cool slightly then pour through clean muslin into clean sterile jars. Ghee should be kept at room temperature otherwise condensation will form in the lid if refrigerated and then brought into a warm room. So long as you always use a clean dry spoon then it will stay fresh and won't spoil.

Breakfasts

Notes

....

....

....

....

The Clover Mill porridge (serves 1)

This is an ideal energy breakfast for vata and pitta types, especially in cold weather. Kaphas or those who wish to avoid gluten (or gliadin – a substance in oats that can mimic the action of gluten in the body) could substitute quinoa flakes or tapioca for the oats.

40 g oats
20 g raisins
20 g slivered almonds
10 g sunflower seeds
Water to cover
Milk (non-homogenised organic dairy, nut, oat or rice milk)
¼ tsp ground ginger
½ tsp mixed spice
¼ tsp ground cardamom – freshly ground seeds taken from pods are best

Soak oats, raisins and almonds in water overnight. In the morning, rinse well, then add ground ginger, mixed spice and ground cardamom and cook gently adding sufficient almond milk (or other milk) to achieve the right consistency.

To make this breakfast even more nutritious and visually pleasing, try adding one or more of the following when serving:

1 tbsp melted coconut oil
1 tsp maple syrup
Toasted seeds
Stewed fruits
Goji berries (hydrate in a little hot water for 2 minutes first)
Sliced bananas

Porridge without oats!

Porridge can be made with virtually any grain or legume and any milk. It's good to have variety in our diets and include as many wholegrains as we can to provide our bodies with the necessary fibre. We now know that it's the bacteria in our large intestine that have the ability to break down soluble fibre into the essential short chain fatty acids which are linked to health-promoting effects, including a reduced risk of inflammatory diseases, diabetes, and cardiovascular disease.

Try the following grains or legumes:

Quinoa, aramanth, rice, buckwheat, mung beans, split mung dahl, buckwheat.

Most benefit from soaking overnight although split mung dahl can be cooked without soaking.

Soak overnight in water and in the morning wash well and cook with water or water mixed with any milk or just the milk.

Whilst cooking you can add:

Raisins, dates, seeds such as sunflower seeds for extra nutrition and some crunch.
Freshly grated ginger, turmeric, or dried spices such as ginger, turmeric, cardamom, cinnamon, nutmeg.

Serving suggestions:

Toasted nuts and/or seeds, coconut flakes.
Seasonal berries.
Goji berries (soak in a little hot water for a few minutes then drain and sprinkle on porridge).

Golden rice porridge (serves 6)

This was served to me in Sri Lanka and it felt so warm and nourishing I had to have a go at replicating when I got home so please enjoy it here.

1 cup rice – I like sona masoori (from your local Asian supermarket)
2 cups water
400 mL coconut milk
1 thumb fresh turmeric, grated, or 1 tsp ground turmeric powder
1 thumb fresh ginger, grated
12 dates, chopped
¼ cup cashew nuts
2 tsp ground cinnamon
¼ tsp ground cardamom

Wash rice well with cold water. Add all ingredients except coconut milk, bring to the boil stirring to prevent rice from sticking to the bottom of the pan. While porridge is simmering, gradually add enough coconut milk to cook the rice and make the right consistency porridge. Delicious!

Notes

....

....

....

....

Fermented mung bean pancakes

After an Indian trip I tried to make dosas but didn't realise they had rice as well as mung beans in their mix and I failed miserably to make the large dosas, just ending up with a sticky mess. So, I tried making the mixture thicker and just adding a tablespoon for each pancake and hence this dish was born.

Makes approx. 24 small pancakes (or hundreds of little blinis, lovely with a pâté)
1 cup mung beans
2 cups water

Soak beans in plenty of cold water in the morning and then before bed rinse them well then blitz with two cups of water, then leave them somewhere warm like next to an Aga or in an airing cupboard to ferment overnight.

Next morning add:

1 tsp turmeric
1 tsp toasted cumin seeds (add 1 tsp ghee to small pan and heat seeds until their fragrance appears – about 2–3minutes).
1 tbsp of ghee
A handful of chopped fresh coriander

Then make into small pancakes using a tiny amount of ghee in a non-stick frying pan. I do three at a time. Serve as in photo as a stack or a swirl with fillings such as:

- Sweet potato mash – either steam cubes of potato or roast whole in a hot (220 °C) oven, peel and mash. Add dash of cider vinegar, ½ tsp turmeric, plenty of freshly chopped dill, a little ghee and a tbsp or two of yoghurt, salt and pepper to taste.

- Avocado – mash avocado with plenty of freshly chopped mint, a splash of lemon juice, salt and pepper to taste.

- Creamed spinach – steam or stir fry in a little ghee, strain, add a little lemon juice, cream or yoghurt, salt and pepper to taste.

- Wilted wild garlic – steam or stir fry in a little ghee, strain, add a little lemon juice, yoghurt, salt and pepper to taste.

- Scrambled eggs – scramble eggs with a little ghee or butter, add freshly chopped herbs, turmeric, salt and pepper to taste.

Sweet version

You can also make them sweet – in the morning add turmeric, fresh ginger and cinnamon, make pancakes and serve with a little maple syrup and/or bananas and non-dairy yoghurt (bananas and dairy shouldn't be mixed).

Coconut pancakes (serves 4)

¼ cup coconut flour
4 eggs (preferably free range, grass-fed)
Splash of nut milk or oat/rice milk
2 tbsp melted coconut oil
½ tsp turmeric
¼ tsp baking powder
¼ tsp salt

Whisk all ingredients together and leave to rest for 10 minutes, consistency of the batter should be quite thick to make an American style pancake. Add a little more milk if required as coconut flour can soak up quite a bit of moisture.

Add a large tablespoon of the batter to a frying pan coated with a little ghee or coconut oil and make small (approx. 10 cm diameter) pancakes – I usually cook three per large frying pan. You can keep them warm in a low oven on a plate covered with a saucepan lid.

Serve with blueberries cooked for a few minutes with a teaspoon of grated fresh ginger and cinnamon powder, or some freshly ground cardamom.

Notes

....

....

....

....

Stewed fruits (serves 4)

The variations of this dish are endless, but our popular recipe is as follows:

8 apples – peeled and chopped
4 dried figs – cut in half
4 dried dates – cut in half
Handful of raisins
Thumb of peeled grated fresh ginger
Nub of peeled and grated fresh turmeric (wear gloves to avoid yellow fingers!)
2 tsp cinnamon (to sweeten)

Add enough water to help fruits cook gently to required consistency and simmer for around 20 minutes. Remember slow gentle cooking is best.

Serve alone or with:

Toasted nuts or seeds
Coconut or other non-dairy yoghurt (don't mix dairy with sour fruits such as apples).
Chia seeds stirred in for at least 10 minutes

And in the unlikely event you have any left over you could use it as the base for a delicious nutritious dessert crumble.

Notes

....

....

....

....

Gut-protecting apple porridge (serves 4)

8 apples
400 mL coconut milk
4 dried dates – cut in half
1 tsp cinnamon (to sweeten)
Thumb of peeled grated fresh ginger
Nub of peeled and grated fresh turmeric (wear gloves to avoid yellow fingers)
1 tbsp chia or camelina seeds
4 tbsp slippery elm powder

Peel and chop apples and add to pan with coconut milk, allow to simmer gently whilst adding rest of ingredients. Add water or more coconut milk as required.

Serve with:

A drizzle of coconut oil
A sprinkle of cinnamon
Toasted coconut flakes

Notes

....

....

....

....

Overnight muesli (serves 6)

2 cups oats
½ cup sunflower seeds
½ cup pumpkin seeds
½ cup raisins
½ cup dates or prunes or figs
½ cup dried apricots
¼ cup goji berries

Add oats and seeds to a large bowl and soak overnight in water.

Add dried fruit to a small bowl and soak overnight in a small amount of water or apple juice.

In the morning rinse oats and add unrinsed fruit and soaking liquid to the oats mixing together well. Add apple juice or water or any milk to make the right consistency.

Serve at room temperature.

Serving suggestions:

Toasted seeds, nuts, coconut, fresh fruit, a small amount of room temperature yoghurt or kefir (if not using apple juice).

Notes

....

....

....

....

Toasted oats muesli (serves 1)

This is a lovely mix that cooks the oats rather than soaking them. It can be made and stored in the fridge dry for a couple of days. In summer pittas will enjoy this rather than a hot porridge.

½ cup oats
1 tbsp coconut oil
1 tbsp mixed seeds – sunflower, pumpkin, sesame, linseed
1 tbsp dried fruit – raisins, dates, prunes, figs, goji berries, apricots
1 tbsp mixed nuts – almonds, walnuts, Brazil, hazelnut
1 tsp cinnamon
1 tsp freshly grated ginger
½ cup yoghurt

Toast oats slowly whilst stirring in a large frying pan, add coconut oil when oats are browned and soft and stir well. Add seeds and nuts and cinnamon and continue to toast until they brown and/or pop. Remove from heat and stir in fruit. At this stage the cooled mixture can be stored for a few days.

Add fresh ginger and yoghurt or milk (dairy or non-dairy such as almond, coconut or oat milk) and mix well. Serve and enjoy.

If prepared fresh, then it will be slightly warm which is good for all doshas and seasons. If stored in the fridge and cold yoghurt added, then add a little hot water or hot milk to bring up to body temperature. Cold foods are harder to digest and may promote ama (toxins).

Notes

....

....

....

Bubble and squeak eggs

This isn't a dish we usually serve to guests as eggs can be hard to digest and not really part of the gentle detox food we serve on retreats. But it is one I have once a week or so. If you feel your digestion is good, do try it.

Grate sweet vegetables such as carrots, parsnips, sweet potatoes, etc, plus peas, small florets of broccoli or cauliflower, sliced courgettes, onions, any vegetables you enjoy. Toss in a little ghee, add cumin and coriander seeds or powder, and cook in a frying pan. Just before they are all tender, make one or two wells and add one or two whole organic eggs and either keep on top of the stove or, if the oven is on, place in the oven for a few minutes until the eggs are cooked.

Serve as they are or:

Sprinkled with toasted nuts and seeds
Add a splash of tamari
Add a drizzle of tahini (as it is or watered down and a little lemon juice)
With a slice of seeded bread, mung bean bread

Notes

....

....

....

....

Soups

Basic stock recipe

Make healthy soups delicious with a bit more care and attention – use a homemade vegetable stock, add some fresh herbs, think about what garnishes will enhance the flavour and attractiveness of the dish. Imagine you are about to serve it to the love of your life – add a little more love, you deserve it too.

You can almost use any vegetables you have in your kitchen; greens will make it bitter though so best avoided. I like to use as a minimum:

3 sticks celery
3 carrots
1 onion (plus skins if you don't mind a dark stock)
1 leek
1 litre water

You could add fresh herbs or spices, but I prefer to leave the flavourings to fit the individual soups.

Add chopped vegetables to the cold water, bring to boil and simmer for around 20 minutes to an hour. Strain and use the liquid.

Don't cook for more than an hour. Simmering for an hour is plenty of time to extract all those delicious flavours, any longer and the flavours can deteriorate making the stock taste bitter.

For a richer flavour – sauté chopped vegetables in ghee or oil, or drizzle with oil and roast in a hot oven (200 °C) for 15 minutes then add to a large stock pot, add water, bring to the boil as above.

The remaining cooked veggies go to our hens who love them.

Notes

Pea and mint soup (serves 4)

1 tbsp ghee or oil
1 tsp cumin seeds
1 small onion
1 cloves garlic
500 g freshly shelled or frozen peas
1 litre water
1 large handful of mint leaves
Salt and freshly ground black pepper to taste

Add cumin seeds to warm oil in a saucepan and cook gently for around 30 seconds until you can smell the cumin – but don't burn them! Add the chopped onion and garlic, stir for a minute, add the peas and water, bring to the boil and simmer until peas are soft.

Add mint and blend to a smooth soup. Return to the heat and add seasoning and more water if required for a creamy soup.

If like here, you often have a glut of courgettes in late summer you can add quite a bit of chopped courgette which improves the texture but doesn't really affect the taste.

Serving suggestions:

Yoghurt and fresh mint leaves
Toasted pumpkin seeds
Pumpkin seed pesto (pound together fresh mint, toasted pumpkin seeds, salt and olive oil in a pestle and mortar). Add a sprinkle of nutritional yeast for extra nutrition and also a slight cheese flavour.

Wild garlic soup – with or without nettles (serves 4)

There is something special about donning gloves, basket and scissors and heading out into the garden to pick food, especially on a sunny spring morning, so this is one of my favourites to make and eat. Often the wild garlic appears before the nettles here and it's delicious on its own too. The leaves smell much stronger than they taste!

A large basket of leaves of wild garlic – best when tender before the flowers appear – if adding nettles then just hold the top four leaves and snip off to not get too much stem. 'Pruned' like this they will keep shooting fresh new leaves all through the summer.

2 tbsp ghee or oil
1 onion
1 leek
3 sticks celery
2 carrots
Approx. 10 large handfuls of nettles and 5 of garlic leaves
1 litre water or homemade stock
Salt and freshly ground black pepper to taste

Heat ghee or oil in a large pan and sweat the chopped onion, leek, celery and carrots until soft – around 10–15minutes. Add stock and wild garlic and nettles and simmer for 5–10 minutes until tender. Blend and reheat but don't let it boil. Check seasoning and consistency and serve.

Serving suggestions:

Freshly ground nutmeg
Swirl of cream – dairy, soy or coconut
Toasted seeds
Wild garlic flowers
Yellow dead nettle flowers look lovely – see photo

Notes

....

....

....

....

Carrot and ginger soup (serves 4)

What better soup to cleanse and detox your whole body? Warming, tasty and good for all dosha types. You could make it richer by adding some coconut milk, tastier by using homemade stock, or simpler by using the standard recipe.

1 tbsp ghee or oil
1 large onion or leek
1 kg carrots
2 sticks celery
1 large thumb of fresh ginger
1 little finger of fresh turmeric or ½ tsp powder
2 litres homemade stock or water
Salt and freshly ground black pepper to taste

Heat ghee or oil in a large pan and sweat onion, carrots, celery, ginger and turmeric. Add stock or water and bring to the boil. Cook until carrots are soft – about 15 minutes. Blend and return to pan. Check consistency and seasoning.

Could add coconut milk to make your soup creamier – good for vata and pitta but not for kapha.

Serving suggestions:

Toasted pumpkin seeds
Freshly grown bean sprouts
Swirl of cream
Fresh coriander
Fresh flowers – nasturtium, marigold

Notes

Roasted leek and fennel soup (serves 4)

1 tbsp ghee or oil
2 tsp fennel seeds
2 fennel heads
2 large leeks
1.5 litres homemade stock or water
Salt and freshly ground black pepper to taste

Roughly slice fennel and leeks and place on large roasting tray. Dot on ghee or sprinkle with oil and fennel seeds and place in hot oven to roast – around 220 °C for 15–20 minutes.

Add to pan with stock or water and bring to the boil. Simmer for 10–15 minutes, blend and return to pan. Check consistency and seasoning.

Serving suggestions:

Swirl of cream
Chopped fresh fennel fronds
Thinly sliced leeks sautéed in ghee
Fresh marigold petals

Notes

Beetroot and apple soup (serves 4)

This shouts out autumn! Strong delicious colour and taste, earthy and fresh from the garden and orchard.

1 tbsp ghee or oil
1 large onion
1 tsp cumin seeds
1 star anise
6 large beetroot (raw)
2 cooking apples – or eating apples plus 1 tbsp cider vinegar
2 litres homemade stock or water
Salt and freshly ground black pepper to taste

Add ghee or oil to a large pan and sweat onion with the cumin seeds for a few minutes. Add chopped beetroot and stir for a few minutes then add stock and bring to boil. Meanwhile core apples and add to pot with star anise. Simmer gently until the beetroot is cooked – about 30 minutes. Discard the star anise and blend soup, returning to pan to check consistency and adjust seasoning.

Variation:

Add a handful of elderberries (use a fork to dislodge from stalks) and simmer for 10 minutes.

Serving suggestions:

Blobs of yoghurt
Freshly chopped mint
Dried apple rings

Mung bean soup (serves 4)

This is a fabulous detoxifying and balancing dish for all doshas. It can be eaten three times a day (yes for breakfast too!) for two–three days to re-set after indulging, or if you're feeling sluggish as it will stimulate digestion, energise and lighten your body.

1 tbsp ghee or oil
1 cup dried mung beans
2 tsp ground coriander
1 tsp cumin seeds
2 cm fresh turmeric or ¾ tsp dried turmeric
1 thumb fresh ginger
¼ tsp asafoetida (ensure gluten-free if required as often mixed with wheat)
2 litres homemade stock or water
Salt and freshly ground black pepper to taste
Fresh lemon juice

Place mung beans in a large pan with plenty of fresh cold water and leave overnight. Next morning rinse well and place in pan with water and bring to the boil. Add turmeric and simmer gently. When cooked – about 20 minutes, add ghee to a small pan and add the asafoetida and sizzle for a few seconds before adding the cumin seeds, coriander and ginger and sizzle until they become aromatic without burning. Add this tarka to the mung beans, simmer for a few minutes, add seasoning and a little fresh lemon juice and serve.

Variations:

Add 1 head fennel sliced and 2 tsp fennel seeds to reduce excess pitta or to add more flavour and texture – don't blend.
Add shredded chard and simmer for 5 minutes
Add coconut milk for a richer soup – not for detox

Serving suggestions:

Sautéed chopped chard stalks
Yoghurt
Lots of chopped fresh coriander or other fresh herbs

Welcome soup (serves 6)

If you've stayed at The Clover Mill you might remember the first night welcoming soup – basic, clear, fresh tasting and warming. You will have learnt that it is vata reducing, rehydrating and delicious. Many first-time guests arrive a little anxious about whether they will be given enough to eat, will they manage the yoga, what do they wear in the steam room and that's after they've negotiated the train journey and been met by the local taxi driver, or navigated their way along country lanes to find us. So, this first course aims to calm, rehydrate and refresh. From around late June to December the veggies are from the garden and are sweet and tasty.

1 leek
3 carrots
5 stems of celery including green tops
1.5 litres water
Salt and freshly ground black pepper to taste
Fresh coriander

Finely chop all vegetables, add to cold water, bring to boil and simmer for 10 minutes. This can be done a little in advance and then brought to the boil just before serving. Add plenty of fresh coriander to serve – you can use the stalks finely chopped too.

Notes

Red lentil and chard soup (serves 6)

500 g red lentils
2.5 litres cold water
2 medium red onions
2 tbsp ghee or coconut oil
200 g Swiss chard
Handful of coriander leaves
2 tsp ground cumin
1 tsp ground cinnamon
1 tbsp coriander seeds
1 garlic clove, crushed
Salt and black pepper to taste

Wash the lentils in plenty of cold water. Place in a large saucepan with 2.5 litres of water, bring to the boil and simmer for 35 minutes or until soft. Skim off any scum that rises to the surface during cooking. Thinly slice the red onions, fry in ghee or oil over a medium heat, stirring occasionally, for 4–5 minutes, until the onions soften and become translucent. Meanwhile, remove and discard the large stems from the Swiss chard. Wash and rinse the leaves thoroughly, then chop them roughly. Do the same with the coriander, leaving a few whole leaves for garnish later. Add the cooked onions, chard leaves and chopped coriander into the lentil soup and season with salt and pepper to taste. Reheat the soup and simmer gently for 5 minutes. Using a pestle and mortar crush the coriander seeds, cumin and cinnamon and garlic together. Warm oil gently in a small saucepan over a medium heat, add the garlic and spice mix and fry for a couple of minutes, until the garlic starts to colour slightly. Stir this into the soup, remove the pot from the stove and cover with a lid. Leave the soup to infuse for 5 minutes before serving. Serve garnished with lemon zest and fresh coriander.

Serving suggestions:

Finely dice a few of the chard stalks and sauté to sprinkle on top to serve.

Sweet Potato and Rosemary Soup (serves 6)

This is a deliciously satisfying and tasty soup, sweet, aromatic and nutritious. Great for a vata pacifying autumn lunch.

6 large sweet potatoes
1 small onion
2 tsp ghee or oil
1 can coconut milk
2 litres stock
Handful of chopped fresh rosemary
Salt and pepper to taste

Roast the potatoes with skins on until tender and caramelised.

Gently fry the chopped onion in ghee or oil, add chopped rosemary, add potato flesh and stir for a few minutes. Add can of coconut milk and stock and break up potatoes a little with a large spoon. Bring to a gentle simmer for 5 minutes. Blend with hand blender or in a processor and serve.

Serving suggestions:

Tamari coated toasted pumpkin seeds (toast seeds in a small pan and sprinkle with tamari)
Chopped rosemary
Drizzle of olive oil

Notes

....

....

....

....

Parsnip and apple soup (serves 6)

2 kg parsnips
½ kg apples
1 large onion
2 tsp ghee or oil
2 litres of stock

Fry chopped onion in ghee or oil and add peeled and chopped parsnips and stir fry for a few minutes. Add stock, apples and bring to the boil. Simmer for 15 minutes or until parsnips are tender.

Use a hand blender or processor to produce a lovely smooth soup – make sure consistency is not too thick or it might resemble apple sauce! You could add a little milk or cream or equivalent if required.

Notes

....

....

....

....

Broccoli and sunflower seed soup

(serves 2 as part of a meal or 1 hungry person)

This is my go-to soup for lunch if I'm pushed for time, really hungry and have broccoli growing. It is delicious, packed full of flavour and nutrients and is filling. It also takes a few minutes to make.

1 head broccoli
½ cup sunflower seeds (ideally soak for a few hours first and rinse)
1 litre of water
1 level tbsp miso or fava bean paste or to taste
Fresh herbs to garnish

Add all ingredients to a Vitamix or processor and blitz, then bring to the boil in a saucepan, simmer for 5 minutes and serve.

Or simmer first and eat as it is or use a food processor or hand blender to blend.

Serving suggestions:

Fresh herbs
Toasted sunflower seeds with tamari
Roasted broccoli pieces
A drizzle of cream (dairy, oat or soy)

Notes

....

....

....

....

Soup garnishes

I love food to look appetising and visually appealing, so we always garnish our soups with something to add colour, nutrition or some crunchy texture. Here are some of our favourites:

Toasted seeds (sunflower, pumpkin, sesame – especially black sesame)
Toasted seeds with a splash of tamari or soy sauce
Toasted coconut flakes
Toasted seaweed flakes
Sumac
Smoked paprika
Flowers
Fresh herbs

Pesto

Pesto is a deliciously tasty oil herb dressing, traditionally made with basil, pine nuts, olive oil and parmesan cheese. But pretty much any fresh herb, seeds such as pumpkin or sunflower make great substitutes.

One of my favourites is to use the green leafy tops of carrots, sunflower seeds, a little nutritional yeast (for cheese flavour), basil and olive oil, salt and pepper.

Try watercress, rocket, kale – be adventurous!

Notes

....

....

....

Pâté and dips

Carrot and Cumin Pâté (serves 4)

This is a great spread to make and take for a packed lunch together with some homemade bread, crackers or mung bean pancakes.

1 tbsp ghee
6 large carrots
2 tsp cumin seeds
2 tbsp live yogurt
1 tbsp lemon juice
Handful fresh coriander
Salt and freshly ground black pepper to taste

Roughly chop carrots and spread over an oven tray. Sprinkle with cumin seeds and ghee and place in hot oven 200–220 °C for 25 minutes.

Blend in a food processor or with a hand stick adding yoghurt, lemon juice, fresh coriander and seasoning to taste.

Serve with homemade bread or crackers

Notes

....

....

....

....

Beetroot and Walnut Pâté (serves 4)

Beetroots are a delicious, tasty source of fabulous nutrients. They are a particularly good source of fibre, iron and folate. Walnuts have the appearance of the brain and its two hemispheres and are packed with DHA, a type of omega-3 fatty acid that does indeed protect the brain from inflammation and ageing. So together they are a great pairing.

1 tbsp ghee
1 tsp cumin seeds
4 medium beetroots
100 g walnuts
Fresh lemon juice
Salt and freshly ground black pepper to taste

Peel and cube beetroots and place on a roasting tray. Sprinkle with cumin seeds, drizzle with ghee and roast in hot oven 200–220 °C for 25–30 minutes.

When beetroot is cooked, sprinkle on walnuts and roast for just 1–2 minutes – keep an eye on them so they don't burn.

Scrape everything including the lovely juices into a food processor and blend leaving some texture if you prefer. Add seasoning and lemon juice to taste.

Serve with homemade bread or crackers, or blinis made exactly the same as mung bean pancakes except smaller, about 4 cm diameter.

Notes

....

....

....

....

Hummus

Hummus is a great dish to have ready in the fridge to have for a light lunch, starter, or a healthy snack. Try adding fresh herbs such as coriander, or substitute some or all of the chickpeas with roasted carrot or beetroot. Tinned chickpeas are fine but if you can, try to use dried as they haven't been processed and so you are in control of the ingredients. They also taste better!

1 cup dried chickpeas
1 tsp bicarbonate of soda

The addition of bicarbonate of soda helps soften the peas and makes for a creamier hummus, but if you prefer it with more texture then omit the bicarbonate of soda.

Soak overnight in plenty of cold water. Rinse and add to a large pan with another tsp bicarbonate of soda and enough cold water to cover peas by about 2 cm. Bring to boil and simmer until well cooked. Skim off any scum and discard. When well cooked, drain and cool.

2 cloves garlic
Juice from 2 lemons
3 tbsp dark tahini
1 tsp ground cumin
Salt and freshly ground black pepper to taste

While cooling, add two peeled garlic cloves to a food processor together with cumin and tahini, add chickpeas and process, adding more lemon juice and seasoning to taste. If you cooked them with bicarbonate of soda then you probably won't need to add any water or olive oil, but I like to add a splash of olive oil for flavour and goodness.

Variations:

Add a handful of fresh coriander and process.
Add a cup or two of roasted carrots or beetroot

Serve with homemade bread or crackers, or for a summer lunch, serve with raw crudités (not for vata).

Notes

....

....

....

....

Sunflower Seed Pâté (serves 4)

This is a quick, simple, highly nutritious and tasty pâté to make.

1 cup sunflower seeds
1 tbsp tahini
1–2 tbsp olive oil
Juice from 1 lemon
1 tsp cider vinegar
Salt and freshly ground black pepper to taste

Soak sunflower seeds in cold water for about two hours.

Add all ingredients to a food processor and process until the required consistency is achieved adding water and/or olive oil.

This pâté can be used to prepare courgette rolls. Use a peeler to produce flat strips of courgette. Sprinkle with salt and leave for 10 minutes then rinse well and pat dry. Lay out strips along a board, add a good teaspoon of pâté to one end, plus a piece of sun-dried tomato and a basil leaf, roll up carefully and serve.

Serving suggestions:

Serve pâté with bread or crackers or if in summer, with raw vegetable crudités (not for vata).

Notes

....

....

....

....

Shitake mushroom pâté (serves 4)

Fresh shitake mushrooms have a delicious flavour and are packed with nutrients such as copper, selenium, B vitamins and beta-glucans. Beta-glucans help support the immune system but also as they pass undigested through to the large intestine, they feed our gut microbiome with necessary fibre so are a prebiotic.

This recipe uses the mushrooms in their raw state so helping us to ingest a few probiotics (good bacteria and yeasts) to support our gut microbiome and helping increase its diversity. Although we don't often eat raw food in Ayurveda, if served at lunchtime in the warmer months and with a warm bread this raw pâté is absolutely fine.

100 g fresh shitake mushrooms
75 g sunflower seeds (soaked in water for 1–3 hours, washed and drained)
2–3 tbsp tamari sauce

Add mushrooms and sunflower seeds to a food processor and process until well chopped but not over-processed. Add tamari to taste.

Lovely eaten with a steaming bowl of soup and served on our seed crackers, warm bread or rotis, or anything really!

Serving suggestions:

With pea shoots pomegranate seeds, tarragon and mustard dressing
On/with warm rotis, bread, crackers

Notes

....

....

....

....

Herby Yoghurt Dip

This is a favourite with our guests, and we serve it with savoury muffins, added as a dollop in soup, or with curries.

Greek yogurt is best, but coconut yoghurt, soya yoghurt can also be used. Add a drop of cider vinegar to these if you prefer a sourer taste.

250 mL yoghurt
Fresh coriander – lots!
Fresh mint – lots!

For four people as a dip, use about 250 mL yoghurt and a generous handful of fresh herbs. Chop the herbs finely by hand and mix into the yoghurt. Don't use a processor as this can make the yoghurt too thin for a dip. If you can, leave it 1–2 hours before eating to allow the flavours to infuse.

Notes

....

....

....

....

Pumpkin Seed Pâté (serves 4)

This is a highly nutritious pâté as pumpkin seeds are full of minerals such as phosphorus, magnesium, manganese, and copper, zinc and iron. Turmeric adds anti-inflammatory properties. This is good for all dosha types.

2 cups pumpkin seeds soaked for 1–2 hours, drained and rinsed
1 tbsp tamari
1 clove garlic (optional)
1 tsp turmeric powder or 1 cm fresh
2–3 sun-dried tomatoes (optional)
Water to blend
Salt and freshly ground black pepper to taste

Add all ingredients except water to a food processor and blend until well mixed. Add water whilst blending until a smooth consistency is reached. Season and serve.

Serving suggestions:

Serve pâté with bread or crackers or if in summer, with raw vegetable crudités (not for vata). This pâté goes well with peppery nasturtium leaves and flowers sprinkled with toasted sunflower or pumpkin seeds.

Notes

....

....

....

....

Raita

Raita is used to add a cooling action to spiced dishes. Cumin seeds are added to help the digestion of dairy or other non-dairy yogurts such as coconut or soy.

Yoghurt can aggravate kapha as it is cold and dense, but the addition of cumin seeds, mustard seeds and asofoetida minimises this so that kapha can eat small amounts occasionally

Whole fat yoghurt (dairy, coconut, soy)
Grated peeled cucumber
Toasted cumin seeds
Toasted mustard seeds
Pinch of asofoetida (optional, not so good for pittas)

Mix well and add sufficient water to make a drinkable consistency. Serve at room temperature.

Notes

....

....

....

....

Savoury snacks, breads and crackers

Notes

....

....

....

....

Seed crackers (Makes 48 so halve quantities if you don't want this many)

These use the magic chia seeds – packed full of fibre, omega 3, calcium and are a great antioxidant. They also form a gel when added to water which can be used as an egg substitute or to bond other ingredients together such as these crackers. Chia seeds are now grown in Essex so buy these rather than from South America. These are a great snack to have in the fridge – store in an airtight container for a few days. They probably won't last that long though!

1 cup pumpkin seeds
1 cup sunflower seeds
1 cup sesame seeds
1 cup chia seeds (or camelina seeds)
2 cups water

Preheat oven to 180 °C, (fan 160 °C), 350F or gas mark 4 or use Aga baking oven.

Add all ingredients to a large mixing bowl, mix well and leave for about 15 minutes.

We then usually add 1 tsp nigella seeds, or cumin seeds, a splash of tamari and salt and freshly ground black pepper to taste. But use your favourite herbs and spices, chopped dulse (seaweed), sundried tomatoes or olives.

Spread mixture onto a silicon baking tray, smoothing edge to edge about 5mm deep. This mix will cover two large trays. Place in the oven for around 20 minutes, then remove and score into appropriately sized crackers – ours are about 5 x 10 cm – and carefully turn over to cook/dry the other side. Or, you can spread into a rough shape, bake, and break into shards, whichever look you prefer.

Serve with:

Any homemade pâté, hummus, nut butter, avocado, scrambled eggs.

Sri Lankan rotis

In Sri Lanka every evening we were served these rotis with a delicious soup. So now each time I smell them cooking I am transported back to sitting outside with the sounds of the sea and tropical cicadas, feeling warm and relaxed from the day's massages. On the cooking course they taught us how to make them.

1 cup kurakkan flour (this is a type of millet i.e. gluten-free and can be bought in Indian shops, or substitute wholemeal flour or GF buckwheat flour)
1/3 cup desiccated coconut
Water
Pinch of salt

Mix together the flour, coconut and salt, then drizzle in enough water to make the dough into a soft ball. Leave to rest for 10 minutes. Flatten the ball on the work surface then with a rolling pin roll to about 3mm thick. Cut into circles with a round cutter. Place in a dry frying pan or on the top plate of an Aga and cook both sides for about 2–3 minutes or until they turn a light brown.

Variations:

Add grated carrot, and/or finely chopped wild garlic leaves to the pastry circle, fold in half and roll out, cut circles etc.

Serve with soup, curry, dips, pâté.

Notes

....

....

....

....

Mung bean and wild garlic bread (serves 8)

This amazingly easy to digest, nutritious, light bread was inspired by Jasmine Hemsley's recipe and is delicious with the addition of a few leaves of wild garlic when in season, otherwise use fresh rosemary.

1¼ cups dried mung beans
2 tbsp olive oil plus drizzle for serving
6–8 wild garlic leaves
1 tbsp chopped rosemary
½ tsp jaggery (sugar)
¼ tsp asafoetida
½ tsp salt
½ cup warm water
½ tsp bicarbonate of soda
Juice of a lemon (about 4 tbsp)
Freshly ground black pepper

Preheat oven to 180 °C, (fan 160 °C), 350 F or gas mark 4 or use Aga baking oven.

Soak mung beans in plenty of water overnight, then rinse well and add to blender. Preferably leave this in a warm place all day or overnight to ferment making it easier to digest. Blend, then add all the other ingredients (except bicarbonate of soda and lemon juice) to the blender and blend briefly. Then quickly mix in bicarb and lemon juice and pour immediately into prepared 20 cm cake tin and place in oven.

Bake the bread in the oven for 25–30 minutes or until lightly brown on top and springy to the touch. Drizzle with olive oil, sprinkle with black pepper and serve. Lovely with soups, pâtés or just olive oil.

Best eaten on the day.

Superseed bread (serves 8)

This is another lovely gluten-free bread that really does supersede supermarket bread. It is good to have occasionally when you feel like something crunchy and filling. This version gives quite a dense loaf that is best eaten on the day you cook it.

1 large sweet potato – about 200 g cooked flesh
110 g buckwheat or yellow pea flour
4 tbsp arrowroot or tapioca flour
1 tbsp ground flaxseeds
½ tsp bicarbonate of soda
2 tbsp lemon juice
½ tsp salt
165 g mixed seeds such as pumpkin, sunflower, chia, sesame

Preheat oven to 180 °C, (fan 160 °C), 350F or gas mark 4 or use Aga baking oven.

Roast the sweet potato for about 45 minutes or until soft. Scoop out flesh and mash with a fork in a large bowl. Add all ingredients and mix well with a silicon spatula or your hands – lightly floured. Shape into an oval or loaf shape with your hands and place on a greased oven tray. Bake for 35–40 minutes until crisp and browned on the outside. Place on wire rack to cool before slicing and eating – try to wait!

Notes

....

....

....

....

Savoury muffins (makes 12 large or 30 mini muffins)

Cumin adds great flavour to these muffins and helps digestion, and the pumpkin seeds add a little crunch. If you don't have pumpkin seeds, sunflower seeds make a good substitute, or use a combination of the two.

80 g unsalted butter, melted and cooled, plus a little for frying (or ghee, or 75 g coconut or sunflower oil)
1 onion, finely diced
2 tsp ground cumin
150 g spinach, finely chopped
250 g plain flour (⅔ sorghum and ⅓ fine polenta or teff or yellow pea flour for GF)
2 tsp baking powder
½ tsp bicarbonate of soda
½ tsp salt
2 eggs (or 1 tbsp chia seeds, 1 tbsp flax seeds and 6 tbsp water)

275 g whole milk yoghurt (or dairy-free yoghurt)
150 g carrots, grated finely
40 g pumpkin seeds

Heat the oven to 200 °C/400F/gas mark 6 and line a muffin tin with 12 paper cases or use mini-muffin silicon trays.

Add a little ghee to a large frying pan and sauté the onion until soft and translucent, about 10 minutes. Add cumin, stir for a minute, then add the pumpkin seeds and cook until they start to pop. Add spinach and stir until wilted and soft. Leave mixture to cool.

In a large bowl, whisk together the flour, baking powder, bicarbonate of soda and salt. In a jug, whisk the melted butter/oil, eggs/substitutes and yoghurt. Pour the wet ingredients over the flour and stir with a spatula until just combined. Fold in the cooled onions and spinach mix, and the carrots. Spoon into the cases and bake for about 15 minutes, until a toothpick comes out clean.

Best eaten on the day as they go dry.

Serve with soups, pâtés, dips. Delicious with herb yoghurt.

Notes

....

....

....

....

Main and side dishes

Kitcheri or kitchadi (serves 8–10)

This is the Ayurvedic staple one-pot nutritious delicious meal. Complimentary mung beans and rice give us our complete protein (remember this to tell your meat-eating friends). Being sweet and astringent tastes, white rice and mung dahl are nourishing to tissues and to our immune system and are light and easy to digest. Before I learnt about Ayurveda, I used to be very snobby about eating white rice and only ate brown but actually, unless you have tip top digestion, white is much easier to digest and therefore easier for us to assimilate its nutrients. Kitcheri can be used to give the digestion a break and is a recommended cleanse – just make a pot first thing and eat for breakfast, lunch and dinner for a few days and you will feel lighter and energised – it really does work, and always amazes me. I like to serve it on the first night of each retreat to reassure guests they will have satisfying tasty meals during their stay and to introduce them to Ayurvedic food.

The variations of grains, rice, spices and vegetables are infinite and it's good to vary vegetables especially if you're eating it for a few days around the equinox or change of season.

2 cups rice – basmati is easy to digest, as is sona masoori – a lovely nutty ancient grain
1⅓ cups split mung dahl (NB don't get confused with chana dahl or split yellow peas)
1 onion
1 tbsp ghee or coconut oil
1 tsp cumin seeds
1 tsp fennel seeds
1 tsp coriander seeds
½ tsp cardamom seeds (fresh out of their pods!)
1 tsp kalonji (also known as black onion, black cumin, Nigella sativa)
1 tsp turmeric
Black pepper
2 tbsp pumpkin seeds (omit in detox version)
1 tin organic coconut milk (omit in detox version)
Braggs amino acids or coconut aminos or tamari
2 large sweet potatoes

Kitcheri can be made in one large pot but when we make it for guests on their first night, we make a deluxe version (!) with pumpkin seeds, coconut milk and sweet potato. Still vata pacifying but not so detoxifying as basic kitcheri. So, then we have one pot for the spice mix, one for the grains, one for sweet potato and another for a green veggie.

Finely dice the onion and fry gently in ghee or coconut oil. Meanwhile, add all the spice seeds to a pestle and mortar and grind to a rough powder. Add this to the onions together with turmeric and a few grinds of black pepper (to enhance absorption of turmeric always add a little black pepper). Fry gently for a few minutes until you can smell the wonderful spice aroma, then add pumpkin seeds, heat for a few minutes, then add a tin of organic coconut milk and a couple of tablespoons of amino acids to taste. Simmer very gently for 15 minutes.

Now wash the grains well by adding them to a large saucepan, add plenty of fresh cold water, stir with your hands and tip out cloudy water. Repeat until water is much clearer – maybe 3–4 times. This removes dust and excess starch. Add approx. twice the depth of water to them, boil and then simmer for around 15–20 minutes until the grains of rice and dahl are soft.

Peel and chop sweet potatoes and cook gently in a small amount of water.

When grains and potatoes are cooked, add together with the onion spice mix. Add lemon juice to taste and serve with a green veggie, lots of fresh coriander and a chutney.

It is good to use our hands to wash the grains as that connects our energies into the food. Each of our fingers represents one of the five elements of life. I find that touching the food before cooking helps bring me to the present moment and gives me time to be grateful for all the hands that have helped grow, nurture, pick and distribute these grains to me in my kitchen today. Having spent a few hours picking rice in hot steamy Borneo years ago I really appreciate the back breaking, soggy feet, exhausting work that's required, let alone the wading barefoot in scorching sunshine job of planting the plants beforehand. So, the next time you simply pluck a packet off the shelf and toss it into your trolley – give the women in Asia a grateful thought.

Notes

....

....

....

....

Superseed tart (serves 6)

Base:

2 cups sunflower seeds
1 cup pumpkin seeds
½ cup shelled hemp seeds
1 tsp black cumin (kalonji) seeds
2 tbsp good oil or olive oil
Salt and pepper to taste

Topping:

Grated carrot or courgette – enough to cover base with 1 cm or more of vegetables.
100 mL dairy, soy or oat cream
A few pumpkin seeds to decorate

Add base ingredients to a food processor and blitz to a crumb. Press into the bottom of a lined cake tin and bake in a hot oven (about 220 °C) for 10 minutes – check a couple of times to ensure it doesn't burn.

Pile seasoned grated vegetables on top, add a drizzle of cream and, using a fork, mix and smooth over. Sprinkle on a few pumpkin seeds and bake at around 160 °C for 45 minutes or until the vegetables are cooked and tender.

Cut into slices like a cake and serve warm.

Notes

....

....

....

....

Notes

Lentil-stuffed chard leaves (serves 4)

This dish came from an old favourite recipe I used to make years ago to stuff large field mushrooms which is delicious. The lentil mix enhances the taste of most vegetables so, looking for novel ways to use more green leafy vegetables for our guests I came up with this one.

I cup red lentils (can use any lentils but red are the easiest to digest)
½ litre of stock – not all added at the beginning
1 onion
At least a level tablespoon of fresh thyme or a tsp dried thyme
Juice and zest of a lemon
4 large chard leaves

Fry the onion in a little ghee or oil, add the well washed lentils and enough stock to cover and bring to the boil. Gently cook, adding more stock if needed. When cooked through, add thyme and lemon juice to taste.

Take some freshly picked large chard leaves and remove the stems from the end of the leaves. Blanch leaves briefly in a pan of boiling stock or water. Add a large spoonful of the lentil mixture onto each leaf and roll up into a package, securing the ends underneath. Place packages in a large ovenproof dish.

Serving suggestions:

Chop the stalks and fry gently, add a few chopped fresh tomatoes (if you're not avoiding nightshades) and simmer for a few minutes. Add the sauce to the dish, heat and serve.

Serve on mashed cauliflower, potato or other vegetable.
Garnish with fresh thyme.

Korma curry (serves 4)

This is a lovely mild dish, comforting for autumn and winter, great for pacifying vata but a bit heavy for kapha so either reduce the amount of cashew nuts or only eat a small amount, pittas and kaphas should have lots of bitter greens with it. Serving with cauliflower rice though, rather than a grain makes it lighter and adds the astringent taste.

Sauce:

½ cup cashews soaked in water for at least an hour up to overnight, drained and rinsed
3 tsp garam masala
⅛ tsp chilli powder – vatas and kaphas can have a little more
2 tsp cumin powder
2 tsp turmeric powder
1 400mL tin of coconut milk
2 tbsp coconut oil
200 mL of vegetable stock – preferably homemade – see soup stock

Vegetables:

2 large sweet potatoes
½ cauliflower cut into florets
500 g spinach or rainbow chard (with stalks cut out)
1 cup frozen peas
1 medium onion
1 clove garlic

Peel and chop sweet potatoes and either roast or steam until tender. While they are cooking, add the sauce ingredients to a food processor and blitz to a smooth paste – the longer you soak the cashew nuts the easier this is.

In a large frying pan add a drizzle of coconut oil and cook onions and garlic until soft and transparent. Add cauliflower florets and cook for a few minutes. Add vegetable stock and cook for another few minutes.

Add sauce to frying pan together with the sweet potatoes, peas and spinach and stir well. Serve when the spinach is wilted.

Serve with rice, cauliflower turmeric/spirulina rice or broccoli rice.

Notes

....

....

....

....

Pumpkin or squash curry (serves 6–8)

We grow lots of squash and pumpkins at the mill – they seem to grow well here. I love the Crown Prince firm flesh, and this is a lovely recipe for it. The key is to cook the sauce and then add the chopped squash and then place in the oven so as not to need to stir to keep from burning otherwise it is easy to end up with soup!

2 onions
2 tbsp ghee or coconut oil
1 large thumb of ginger
3 stalks lemongrass
2 tsp ground turmeric or a thumb of fresh
1 tsp ground cumin
2 tsp freshly ground cardamom
1 tsp ground coriander
½ tsp black pepper
Salt to taste
400mL vegetable stock
1.5 Kg diced squash
1 400mL tin of coconut milk
Juice of 1–2 limes
Handful of fresh mint leaves
Handful of fresh coriander leaves

Cook chopped onions in oil until soft and transparent. Peel and finely shred ginger and add together with finely sliced core of the lemongrass stalks and cook. Stir in ground spices. Add coconut milk, stock and stir well. Add chopped squash, place lid on pan and place in the oven to cook – about 160 °C for an hour for flavours to incorporate.

Stir in lime juice, mint and coriander, check seasoning and serve.

Serve with cauliflower rice or basmati or sona masoori rice and sprinkle with more fresh herbs.

Beetroot curry (serves 6 as a side dish)

Beetroot is one of my all-time favourite vegetables and I love it pretty much any way it's cooked, but this curry is quite delicious.

1.5 kg beetroot
2 tbsp grated fresh ginger
2 tsp garam masala (every Indian mother has her own mix – we use one very kindly supplied by one of our guests)
2 tsp ground cumin
2 tsp ground coriander
1 tsp ground turmeric
1 can of coconut milk
½ cup red lentils, washed and drained
Plenty of spinach or rainbow chard, washed and chopped
2 tbsp coconut oil
2 onions
1 tbsp fresh curry leaves
1 tbsp lemon juice
Salt and black pepper to taste
Fresh coriander to serve

Peel and chop beetroot into small chunks and place in a large bowl. Add ginger, garlic, spices and coconut milk to the bowl and mix well to coat the beetroot. Heat coconut oil in a large pan and cook the chopped onion and curry leaves, stirring until browned. Add beetroot mixture, lentils and a cup of water. Stir well and simmer for at least an hour or until beetroot is tender. This dish is best cooked slowly and for longer if you can. Just before serving, season to taste, add spinach or chard, lemon juice, and serve sprinkled with fresh coriander.

Notes

....

....

....

Courgette and dill fritters (makes 6–8 fritters)

I love fresh dill, and this is a great combination of dill, courgette and eggs. Dill improves the appetite by kindling agni and helps digestion by its action on vata. It is carminative (gas reducing), anti-inflammatory, a good brain tonic and clears ama and kapha, amongst other actions.

1 tbsp ghee or coconut oil or sunflower oil
1 medium red onion
2 medium courgettes
2 tsp dill seed
2 tbsp dill fronds
2 tsp chopped parsley
75 g feta cheese (optional but delicious!)
2 tbsp green pea flour or wholemeal flour
2 eggs
Salt and freshly ground black pepper to taste

Heat oil in a large pan and fry the finely chopped onion until soft and translucent. Grate the courgettes and blot with paper to remove excess water. Add to the onion together with the dill seed and cook for 2–3 minutes.

Whisk eggs, flour, feta, parsley and dill fronds together in a bowl, season well, add contents of frying pan and mix well. Wipe pan with paper and add a little oil. Add a large tablespoon of mix to the pan and fry gently on each side for 5–10 minutes until cooked through. Serve straight away or keep warm in the oven until they are all cooked.

Notes

....

....

....

....

Sweet potato and mung bean curry (serves 4)

1½ cups mung beans
4 medium size sweet potatoes, peeled and cut into small chunks
1 tbsp black mustard seeds
1 tbsp cumin seeds
2 tsp garam masala
1 tbsp ghee or coconut oil
1 tsp turmeric powder or 2 tsp grated fresh turmeric
½ tsp freshly ground cardamom
1 tsp cumin powder
1 dried chilli
Salt and black pepper to taste
½ cup of yoghurt or coconut milk

Peel and chop sweet potatoes. Dry roast seeds in a small pan until fragrant and popping, then grind with a pestle and mortar. Heat coconut oil in a large pan and add seed mix and potatoes and mix well. Add garam masala, turmeric, cumin and cardamon powders, chilli and a little salt. Stir for a few minutes then add about 8 cups water and the washed mung beans. Cover and simmer for about 35 minutes until the potatoes and beans are tender. Don't overcook or the beans will lose their shape and colour. When done remove from the heat. Then just before serving stir in yoghurt, sprinkle with plenty of fresh coriander and serve with rice, quinoa or cauliflower rice.

For extra goodness, stir in leaves of swiss chard, beetroot tops or spinach to cook for a few minutes before serving.

Notes

....

....

....

....

Notes

Beetroot burgers (makes 8 large burgers)

I love surprising the guests by serving burgers and mash! But beetroot instead of meat, and mashed celeriac or cauliflower instead of potato. Packed full of fibre, anti-inflammatory goodness, vitamin K, iron and folate.

1 large onion
2 cloves garlic
2 400ml cans of black beans or 3 cups of dried beans, soaked overnight, washed, drained and cooked in water
1 large beetroot
½ cup chickpea (besan) flour
2 tbsp nutritional yeast
1 large handful fresh basil
2 tsp sea salt

Preheat oven to 180 °C.

Add onion and garlic to a food processor and pulse to chop roughly, add peeled and grated beetroot and the rest of the ingredients and pulse a few times, don't overmix.

Either form balls of the mixture and press down onto a greased or silicon baking tray, or I use an 80mm steel cooking ring. Using a spoon and a fork, place mixture into the ring on a greased or silicon tray and press mixture down gently to level with the fork, carefully remove the ring and repeat the process.

Place in oven and bake until cooked – about 30 minutes.

We serve on a bed of cauliflower or celeriac mash, top with avocado mint sauce and serve with a green vegetable such as pak choi, broccoli or kale.

Beetroot risotto (serves 4)

Mint, feta cheese and beetroot are a marriage made in heaven as they say. The earthy flavour of beetroot is lightened with the sour taste of feta and the sweet flavour of mint brings it all together. This isn't a traditional risotto packed with butter and parmesan cheese (sorry!), it's a lighter, easier to digest, more nutritious version, fresh and delicious.

I medium onion
1 tbsp ghee or coconut oil
4 medium beetroots
2 garlic cloves
250 g organic white or brown arborio rice
1 litre of vegetable stock
200 g frozen peas
2 handfuls of freshly chopped mint
200 g feta cheese (optional, pittas will love the sour taste but try not to eat it every day!)

Peel and chop beetroot and roast with a little ghee or oil in a hot oven around 220 °C for around 30 minutes or until they are tender.

Fry the chopped onion in ghee or oil in a large pan until the onion is soft. Add chopped garlic and washed rice and stir for another couple of minutes. Add stock little by little until the rice has absorbed all of it and is soft, note if using brown rice, it might take longer, even up to an hour to become fully soft. Add cooked beetroot either when the rice is cooked or a few minutes before, this will give the dish a beautiful colour. Only cook the peas in a little water and add them at the last minute or they will lose their vibrant colour. Then add feta, mint and serve sprinkled with some of the mint.

Notes

....

....

....

Cabbage subji (serves 4)

In Ayurveda the preferred method of cooking vegetables has always been to either to sauté them slowly in ghee or oil and spices or to cook them with spices in a small amount of water. Modern research shows that green vegetables lose their B vitamins if steamed or boiled and the addition of a little ghee or oil helps retain them. Raw greens can't be digested until they reach our large intestine packed with good bacteria that can breakdown the vegetable fibre for us. Raw vegetables and salads are best eaten only in warm weather at lunchtime during pitta time (10 am – 2 pm), otherwise most of us find them too hard to digest – even if in smoothies. Some nutrients are bound to cell walls and require cooking to release them for us to assimilate. So try to always eat your vegetables cooked.

Subji means a vegetable dish, sometimes called bhaji.

The addition of turmeric, asafoetida and salt help reduce the qualities of cabbage that increase vata, but vata should eat it in moderation, great for pitta and kapha.

1 medium cabbage
2 tbsp oil or ghee
½ tsp black mustard seeds
½ tsp cumin seeds
A pinch of asafoetida (hing)
¼ tsp turmeric
¼ tsp salt
¼ tsp black pepper

Heat a frying pan on medium heat and add oil, mustard seeds, cumin seeds, asafoetida and turmeric and sauté until the seeds pop. Add shredded cabbage, salt and pepper, stir and cover with lid. Simmer on a low heat until cabbage is tender but not overcooked, about 5–8 minutes. Add a drop of water if required to help cook the cabbage.

Notes

Stuffed butternut squash

This is a really simple, delicious dish. Most of the time is waiting for the squash to cook. It can be prepared a little ahead of time and then popped in the oven to warm at the last minute making it an easy but impressive and tasty dish to serve to friends.

Allow ½ medium butternut squash per person

2 medium butternut squash
2 large leeks
1 tbsp ghee or coconut oil
2 tsp fennel seeds
½ cup desiccated coconut
1 cup yoghurt – dairy or non-dairy
Salt and black pepper to taste
Fresh coriander to serve

Preheat oven to 220 °C

Halve squash lengthways and place cut side up on a baking sheet. Roast until tender: 30–45 minutes depending on size and freshness of the squash – when they are straight from our garden they cook more quickly.

While the squash are cooking, fry sliced leeks in a pan with oil or ghee and fennel seeds. When tender, stir in coconut and yoghurt and simmer really gently. You might need to add a splash of water or stock if too dry.

When the squash are cooked, remove seeds with a spoon and then with a knife, cut gently around the edges about 1 cm in from the skin, remove flesh with a spoon and place in the pan with the leek mixture, mix well and season. Spoon this mixture back into the squash shells and return to oven for 5–10 minutes to warm through. Sprinkle with fresh coriander to serve.

Serve alone or with a green veggie, cauliflower rice, or quinoa.

Notes

Asparagus soufflés (makes 6 small ramekins)

These make a lovely spring starter drizzled with fresh tarragon dressing. They have the consistency of a light airy soufflé without the problem of collapse. Tarragon is a perennial herb that usually appears early in the year in our herb garden. Asparagus grows well here too and if you turn your back it's two feet tall so needs to be checked every day.

250 g asparagus
2 whole eggs and 2 egg yolks
125 mL soya cream or dairy cream
¼ tsp turmeric
Salt and black pepper to taste

Heat oven to 160 °C

Chop asparagus stalks and cook in boiling water for just a few minutes until just tender but not overcooked. Rinse in cold water, pat dry with kitchen paper and add to a food processor bowl. Blitz with the eggs, egg yolks, turmeric and seasoning. Add cream and just pulse once. Pour mixture into greased ramekins and place in a bain marie. In other words, place in a large baking dish and fill (carefully without splashing water into the soufflés) with hot water and place in oven until risen, slightly brown on top and set.

You can turn them out onto a warm plate and serve drizzled with tarragon dressing or serve in the ramekins.

Either way they are lovely served alone or with a few extra beautifully cooked asparagus spears.

Roasted vegetable quinoa (serves 4)

Quinoa is a wholegrain that is a complete protein so this dish can be a whole meal in itself. Quinoa is easy to digest and light on the system and suits everyone. Quinoa can be soaked overnight first or cooked straight after washing.

1 cup quinoa
2½ cups water or stock
4 cups chopped mixed vegetable such as onions, courgette, asparagus
1–2 tbsp ghee or coconut oil
A few sprigs of fresh thyme
Salt and black pepper to taste
1 tsp ground cumin
2 tbsp lemon or lime juice
1 tbsp pine nuts lightly toasted by placing in small pan and heating gently – don't stop watching though or they might burn! And omit or reduce if kapha.
1 tsp olive oil
Handful of fresh herbs such as parsley, oregano, marjoram, basil

Preheat oven to 200 °C.

Place chopped vegetables in a roasting pan, toss with ghee or oil and thyme, salt and pepper. Roast for 15–20 minutes or until just soft.

Add quinoa and stock to a pan, bring to the boil and simmer gently for 12 minutes, drain and add to the vegetables (in roasting dish) when they are cooked. Add the lemon or lime juice, ground cumin, pine nuts, drizzle of olive oil, mix well and sprinkle with fresh herbs to serve.

Notes

....

....

....

Cauliflower or broccoli rice (serves 4–6)

This is a great way of serving a vegetable alternative to rice or another grain such as quinoa.

1 head cauliflower or broccoli
1 tbsp ghee or coconut oil
½ tsp turmeric powder or 1 tsp fresh turmeric finely grated
¼ tsp spirulina powder

Simply grate or food process florets of cauliflower or broccoli, or both together. Sauté in a little ghee or coconut oil and cook gently for 10–15minutes until it tastes cooked and is tender, but not overcooked.

Add some freshly grated turmeric, or turmeric powder for a beautiful colour and added anti-inflammatory benefit, and we often add a pinch of spirulina too. Spirulina gives an interesting (!) green colour and is strong tasting but gram for gram is the most nutritious item we can eat, so adding a little into vegetables like cauliflower that are strong enough to hold their own taste is a great idea. You can also use blue spirulina which has the advantage of no taste but doesn't contain the full range of nutrients that the green does. But useful if you want blue and don't like the taste!

The astringent and cooling tasted of cauliflower and broccoli are a great match to sweet, warming curries such as the korma or squash curry.

Notes

....

....

....

....

Vegetable mash – potato alternatives

The more vegetables we can eat each day the healthier we become – it is well established now. The more variety the greater diversity our gut microbiome will have too and as this is being linked to so many different medical conditions as diverse as autism, depression, arthritis and diabetes, it's maybe time to take note and love your veggies. On average during our five–night retreats we serve over 20 different vegetables.

So, a delicious way to serve many root vegetables, cauliflower or broccoli is as a mash. And mashed vegetables are easy for everyone to eat – especially the elderly and the young.

Cauliflower mash or broccoli mash – break into florets and steam gently until tender. Drain and put back into the dry pan on a gentle heat, shaking to allow steam to be released and cauliflower dried off. Then use a hand blender to get the best mash, add a little ghee or coconut oil, salt and black pepper to taste. You could add a little nutritional yeast for a cheese flavour, turmeric for colour and all the benefits of turmeric too.

Sweet potato mash – best to roast potatoes in their skins if you have time, this way the potato sugars caramelise to increase the gorgeous sweet flavour. Or simply peel, cube and steam, and mash as above.

Celeriac mash – peel the celeriac, cut into chunks and either roast on a baking tray in a hot oven, or steam and mash as above. Plenty of black pepper and a little ghee make this a beautiful smooth mash with a delicate celery flavour. Delicious with our beetroot burgers.

Other vegetables to try are:

Carrot and swede – lovely with cumin added whilst mashing.
Peas – maybe keep some texture by using a fork or a potato masher rather than a hand blender, add plenty of fresh mint too.

Roasted vegetables

Another way of serving vegetables is by slowly roasting them. This keeps in all the goodness – I'm sure you've all noticed the amazing green/blue water you're left with after steaming purple sprouting broccoli or bright purple from beetroot, orange from carrots. Roasting keeps all of the nutrition in the vegetable, nothing is lost. In fact, some of the B vitamins in green vegetables are released more when roasting in oil than when eaten raw.

It's very easy to roast vegetables, but as you're using a very hot oven you do need to keep an eye on them and as anyone with an Aga or range will know – that's not so easy (no glass oven doors) and they are easily forgotten!

Florets

Break into florets or cut into chunks, spread onto a baking tray, dress with a little coconut oil or ghee, sprinkle over cumin powder, coriander, turmeric, whichever flavour you enjoy, and roast for 10–15 minutes until tender. Be careful not to burn the tender ends of broccoli.

Whole

Or you can roast a whole cauliflower or broccoli as an impressive addition to your dinner table. Baste with oil or ghee, cover in foil and roast until tender and then remove and baste again with cumin, salt, pepper, turmeric and return to the oven for a few minutes. A sprinkle of smoked paprika or sumac looks great on cauliflower and tastes good too.

Remember all culinary herbs and spices except chilli are great to help your body process and digest food. So, sprinkle them on whenever you can.

You could also make your roasted vegetable, such as cauliflower or beetroot, the main dish by serving it as a steak with a delicious tahini dressing.

Sauces and chutneys

Apple and ginger chutney

This is a recipe from my mum's book on jams and preserves and homemade sweets written in 1969. I use fresh ginger which wasn't easily available in those days.

1 kg cooking apples, peeled and cored and chopped
400 mL water
3 large onions, peeled and chopped
100 g peeled and freshly grated ginger
250 g raisins
2 chopped bananas
350 g unrefined soft brown sugar
½ tsp salt (rock or sea)
Pinch of cayenne pepper
2 tsp mixed spice
500 mL cider vinegar

Add apples, water, onions, ginger, raisins and bananas to a large heavy-bottomed pan. Cover and simmer gently until apples are soft. Add all remaining ingredients and simmer without a lid until the mixture is thick enough. Pour into sterile jars and add lids.

Notes

....

....

....

....

Avocado sauce

This is a thick mayonnaise-consistency sauce we serve with our beetroot burgers (see photo with the beetroot burger recipe) but equally delicious with roasted vegetables, or any vegetable fritter, carrot seeded tart etc.

Blend the flesh of a ripe avocado with a couple of tablespoons of the set part of a tin of coconut milk (it's a great idea to always keep a tin in the fridge for this use), a handful of fresh mint, a few drops of lemon juice, salt and black pepper to taste. This needs to be made just before serving as the mint seems to encourage to avocado to discolour.

Tahini sauce

Another delicious simple sauce to add great nutrition and flavour to a simple roast vegetable dish, seeded breads, pancakes, just try it and see.

In Ayurveda the sesame seed is revered for its oil and its nutritional and medical benefits. They promote longevity and are seen anti-ageing. They are good for our hair and teeth, strengthen the body, increase intelligence and also improve our digestive power. Wow!

Blend a few teaspoons of tahini (dark tahini if you prefer more flavour) with a little water to a pouring consistency. Add a couple of teaspoons of lemon juice to taste.

Notes

....

....

....

Courgette sauce

A lovely fresh sauce to make the most of the summer courgette glut gardeners always have for a few weeks. Simply blitz a whole courgette, lemon juice, olive oil, a handful of fresh mint and a little water if required. Delicious served with roasted vegetables, muffins or fritters.

Tarragon dressing

This is a dressing I've been making for years and is particularly delicious served with the asparagus soufflés.

50 mL virgin olive oil
25 mL cider vinegar
1 tsp honey
1 tsp wholegrain mustard
1 handful freshly chopped tarragon (or 2 tsp dried)

Mix and adjust honey to taste – should be sharp and sweet with a wonderful tarragon flavour. Best made a couple of hours before use.

Notes

....

....

....

....

Cherry and orange chutney

If you like fresh cherries then you will love this fresh chutney, it's not a traditional English chutney made with vinegar to last the winter, but a fresh vibrant chutney made with cherries fresh from the tree and lots of freshly chopped mint from the garden – a burst of late summer goodness. In Ayurveda, chutneys are used as an accent to meals to add digestion and to ensure all six tastes are in every meal.

This recipe is modified from the amazing Maya Tiwari's book – *Living Ahimsa.*

2 cups of fresh large dark cherries, stoned
1 tangerine, peeled and chopped
1 handful chopped fresh mint leaves
1 tsp ground cinnamon
1 tsp freshly ground cardamom (split pods to remove seeds and grind with a pestle and mortar – inhale deeply – what an amazing smell . . .)
½ tsp turmeric
¼ tsp freshly ground black pepper
¼ tsp salt (rock or sea)
1 tbsp homemade ghee
½ tbsp maple syrup

If you haven't got a cherry stoner then simply cut each cherry in half with a small sharp knife and prize out the stone. If they are nice and ripe, they should come out quite easily.

Add all ingredients to a pan and cook on a low gentle heat for about 15 minutes. Cool and store in a glass jar in the fridge until used – 2–3 days.

I love this for breakfast on its own, with coconut pancakes or with warm porridge. And equally lovely with quinoa roasted vegetables.

Damson chutney

This recipe is based on one in my mum's book on jams, preserves and homemade sweets written in 1969. This was before fresh ginger was readily available in the UK and when sugar featured as a major ingredient in any chutney, jam or dessert.

Side benefits of making jam or chutney is the mindful meditation and steaming facial you get whilst picking out the stones...

Choose a sunny day in October when the fruit is ripe, and you have a whole day to indulge in chutney making – you will need it! Start by donning wellies and a scarf – find your favourite basket and scour the hedgerows for trees dripping with dark blue-black fruit with a matt bloom. The leaves of the trees might just be starting to turn autumn yellow. Ripe fruit will come off the tree easily, leaving the stalk behind, but if not, just pick off the stalks before you drop into the basket as this saves time later on.

1.6 kg washed damsons
2 red onions
2 cloves garlic
300 g raisins
250 g dates, stoned
700 g unrefined soft brown sugar
1 litre cider vinegar
2 tsp salt (rock or sea)
2 thumbs of fresh ginger, peeled and finely grated
2 tsp mixed spice
1 tsp freshly ground cardamom
1 tsp turmeric, ground or 2 tsp freshly grated

Chop onions, garlic, raisins and dates. Mix with rest of ingredients in a large heavy bottomed pan – I use my enormous Le Creuset pan. Simmer very slowly for around 2 hours or until the required consistency is attained, removing as many of the stones as you can as they float to the surface. Sterilise jam jars by running them through a hot dishwashing cycle or, if you have the convenience of an Aga, leave them in the simmering oven for an hour with their lids. I use a jug to pour the hot chutney into jars and firmly screw their lids on.

Leave to cool and label.

Notes

....

....

....

....

Fresh ginger chutney

This uses the tart zingy ume plum seasoning, or you can use rice vinegar or cider vinegar. It's a great chutney to have a teaspoon of before meals to enhance agni. You can make in the morning and use all day and, kept in the fridge, should be OK for 2–3 days, if you can resist it that long.

4 tbsp ume plum seasoning (or cider vinegar, or lime)
½ cup freshly grated, peeled ginger
1 tsp rock or sea salt – I like Himalayan best
1 pinch unrefined sugar (coconut, jaggery or rapadura)

This really enhances kitcheri and soup, especially for pittas as we love the spicy, sour, saltiness it gives – but don't have too much!

Notes

....

....

....

....

Desserts

Baked spiced apples (for 1 apple/person)

I love the autumn when I can pop out into the garden and pick apples to bake for dinner. There is something so basic about picking food to eat there and then. This is a quick and easy dish to prepare and pop in the oven to cook whilst you are making the main course.

You can use cooking or dessert apples – cookers will need a bit more sweetener.

1 tsp ground almonds or any chopped nuts
1 tsp raisins or dates
¼ tsp ground cinnamon
¼ tsp mixed spice
½ tsp grated fresh ginger or ½ ball of stem ginger
3–5 tbsp apple juice or water
1 tsp ghee

Preheat oven to 180 °C or use Aga baking oven.

Wash and core an apple per person. Mix ingredients above except for juice and ghee. Stuff ingredients into the apple cavity, top with ghee and place in an oven-proof dish. Pour juice around the apple, cover with foil and bake until soft, basting a couple of times with the juice. Depending on the size of the apple, takes about 45 minutes.

Notes

....

....

....

....

Poached pears (serves 6)

This is a lovely dessert to complete a meal – just a small serving and not too sweet, but flavoursome and satisfying. Although pears are available all year round now in our supermarkets, if you can find a local tree then all the better to look forward to enjoying them in the autumn.

6 ripe pears – conference, comice, or your favourite variety
1 tbsp freshly grated ginger
2 tsp ground cinnamon
4 dates
Juice and zest of 1 large orange
50 mL water

Peel pears leaving on the stalk. Remove a little of the hard core and straighten off the base. Place in a pan with all ingredients and simmer slowly for about 45 minutes or until pears are soft all the way through. Remove pears, mash dates and ginger into the liquid and simmer to reduce to a thick sauce consistency, strain and pour over pears placed upright on individual serving plates. Serve alone, with a dollop of ginger cream, or a piece of homemade biscotti.

Ginger cream

Simply add chopped stem ginger and a tiny drizzle of syrup to cream, or non-dairy soy cream, Oatley crème fraiche or natural yogurt, etc.

Notes

....

....

....

....

Biscotti

This biscuit is twice baked and so it is crunchy – it is meant to be served with coffee or a glass of fortified wine, but it is also delicious served with the poached pear in the sauce described earlier.

This can be made gluten-free. Fennel seeds aid digestion and help to cleanse our breath making this biscuit perfect for ending a meal with.

1 egg and 1 egg white
100 g jaggery, turbinado or coconut sugar
1 tsp vanilla paste
1 tbsp melted ghee
150 g chopped almonds
1 tsp baking powder
250 g wholemeal flour such as spelt. For gluten-free we use 75 g rice flour, 75 g fine polenta, 50 g yellow pea flour, 50 g buckwheat flour
Zest of 2 oranges
2 tsp fennel seeds
1 tsp ground cinnamon

Whisk egg, egg white and sugar together in a large bowl. Add vanilla paste and ghee. Mix together the dry ingredients and stir into the eggs to give a soft dough. Shape into a log about 5 cm wide and 2.5 cm high and bake at 160 °C for about 35 minutes or until firm and golden.

Cool slightly, slice diagonally about 1 cm thick and place on baking tray cut side up. Cook for another 20 minutes or so until golden, turning over each piece after 10 minutes. Leave to cool and store in an airtight container.

Notes

....

....

....

Chia coconut pudding (serves 6)

This is a rich nutritious dessert – you don't need a large amount. The wonderfully nutritious and versatile chia seed is from the mint family and is now grown in the UK as are camelina seeds which are from the broccoli family and known as Gold of Pleasure. They are both high in protein, fibre and omega 3 and can also be used as egg substitutes for vegans.

400 mL coconut milk – tinned or a carton
4 tbsp chia or camelina seeds
1 tsp ground cinnamon
4 medjool dates (or dried dates soaked in hot water for a few minutes then drained)

Process dates in a food processor then add coconut milk and process until smooth, add seeds and cinnamon and pulse for just a few seconds until well mixed. Leave to sit for around 30 minutes then stir or process for a few seconds to ensure a consistent mixture.

Place in glasses or small bowls to serve.

Serving suggestions:

Add layer of fruit coulis
Sprinkle with toasted coconut flakes
Sprinkle with grated high-quality chocolate

Notes

....

....

....

....

Gogi dessert (serves 6–8)

Sometimes I challenge guests to guess all the ingredients in this unusual, deliciously tasty dessert, offering them a free weekend if they guess correctly – confident I am that nobody would be able to guess every single one! Now this book is out I will have to stop the fun!

1 cup cashew nuts – soaked for 1–2 hours, washed and drained
1 cup goji berries – soaked for 1–2 hours, washed and drained
½ cup maple syrup
1 tablespoon lemon juice
1 teaspoon lemon zest
1 teaspoon vanilla paste
1 thumb fresh ginger
1 fresh orange, peeled
¼ cup coconut oil
1 tbsp chia seeds
1 tbsp maca powder

Place goji berries into food processor and process until smooth. Add all remaining ingredients and process again until smooth. Pour into glasses or bowls to serve.

Top with:

Coconut cream
Toasted coconut flakes
A few whole goji berries
A few slithers of stem ginger

Raw chocolate mousse torte

This is a highly nutritious, rich dish, so serve small portions and only occasionally!

Be aware that serving in the evening might keep you awake if, like me, you find raw cacao energising! We often serve this as a treat to guests on their last day with us to help them focus on their journey home.

Base:

150 g ground almonds
100 g raisins
3 knobs of stem ginger
1 tsp ground ginger
1 tbsp coconut oil

Mousse:

2 large ripe avocados
75 g raw cacao powder
50 g melted coconut oil
50 g coconut sugar
1 tsp vanilla paste
1 pinch of salt

Line a spring form cake tin with foil.

Process all base ingredients until roughly chopped and combined – be careful not to process to a paste, keep some texture. Press into cake tin and place in the fridge while you make the filling. Wipe processor bowl with kitchen roll, no need to wash.

Add all ingredients to the food processor bowl and process until well-mixed and smooth. Adjust sugar and salt according to taste. Pour/scoop onto base, level off top and place in fridge for at least 4 hours to set.

Serving suggestions:

Because this is so rich, the addition of fresh raspberries, strawberries, blueberries or other seasonal berries definitely enhance this dish.

Fragrant rice pudding

Rice pudding often splits the crowd – those who suffered lumpy school servings and those of us who loved our mother's homemade version. My great Auntie who used to (coincidentally) live up the road from the mill used to make one every day after breakfast and leave it to cook slowly in their old wood-fired Rayburn. Made with creamy local milk it had a delicious skin on it covered in nutmeg, it was my favourite.
My version is a bit healthier but still creamy tasting with the coconut milk and eggs and the addition of fragrant with spices help us to digest it. If you're vegan, then the egg yolks can just be left out.

1 vanilla bean pod
3 cloves
2 cardamom pods (crushed)
1 stick cinnamon
3 cups coconut milk
1 tbsp maple syrup
½ tsp lime zest and you'll need another ½ teaspoon lime zest
200 g pudding rice (short grain rice) or risotto rice
2 egg yolks (optional)

Heat oven to 160 °C

Lightly toast vanilla seeds and pod, cloves, cardamom pods, and cinnamon stick broken in half. Just a couple of seconds in a small pan on the hob.

Heat coconut milk, cream and ½ teaspoon of lime zest to almost boiling. Add the rice and bring to a gentle simmer for 3–5 minutes, then remove from the hob.

In a separate bowl whisk the egg yolks and add into the rice pudding, stir until thickened and pour into an ovenproof dish. Sprinkle ½ teaspoon of lime zest on top and bake at 200 °C.

Place in the oven for 30–60 minutes to finish cooking slowly.

Gluten-free fruit crumble (serves 4–6)

I've always liked to add oats and seeds to my fruit crumbles for extra fibre, flavour and texture. This recipe is a great topping for pretty much any fruit combination you have. At The Clover Mill we love to use mulberries when the birds kindly leave us a few, damsons during October and November and apples from October onwards. We only serve a small amount as it is sweet and relatively heavy to end a meal. In Ayurveda it is said to 'eat fruit alone or leave fruit alone', however this generally refers to raw fruit and so a little cooked fruit is OK.

Fruit:

Apples – peel, core and slice cooking or eating apples. Place in a pan with a little water or apple juice, ground cinnamon, fresh ginger and simmer gently until soft.
Berries – no prior cooking required

Crumble topping:

100 g ground almonds
50 g buckwheat flour
50 g rice flour
250 g oats (I prefer jumbo organic)
50 g sunflower seeds
25 g sesame seeds

Preheat oven to 180 °C.

Add topping ingredients to a food processor and blitz until well mixed, drizzle in 3 tbsp coconut or light olive oil. Spread onto fruit, sprinkle with seeds, dot with ghee and bake for 20–30 minutes until golden.

Serving suggestions:

Ginger cream is delicious on most crumbles, or any dairy or non-dairy cream.

Notes

....

....

....

....

Baobab and lemon mousse cake

This is a highly nutritious, rich dish, so serve small portions and only on special occasions! Baobab powder adds a fruity depth to the flavour of the mousse – you can substitute with lucuma powder, maca, or simply omit if you don't have any. However, it's a great source of vitamin C, B6, iron, magnesium and calcium plus is a good source of fibre for our gut microbiome. To get a smooth, light topping you will need a Vitamix type processor.

Base:

1 cup ground almonds
1/3 cup coconut flakes
½ cup raisins or medjool dates
2 tbsp melted coconut oil

Filling:

3 cups cashew nuts (soaked overnight, washed and drained)
¼ cup almond or coconut milk
Zest of 1 lemon
Juice of 4–5 lemons – about 8 tbsp
¾ cup maple syrup
2 tbsp baobab powder
1 cup melted coconut oil

Line a spring form cake tin with foil. Process base ingredients together until well combined but still plenty of texture. Press mixture into the tin and place in fridge.

Place all ingredients for the filling except the coconut oil into a Vitamix or equivalent. Process until mixed and creamy, then add warmed coconut oil and mix well. Be careful not to mix for too long otherwise mixture will get too hot and will destroy the vitamin C. Pour into the tin and refrigerate until set – at least 4 hours.

Decorate with seasonal berries and fresh lime zest and serve cut into (small!) slices.

Coconut panna cotta with fruit coulis

400 mL coconut milk
400 mL almond milk
25 g unrefined caster sugar
1 vanilla pod
Gelatin sheets or vegetarian gelling powder
300 g mulberries or other fruit
2 tbsp maple syrup
1–2 tsp lemon juice

Add milks to a pan together with the sugar and split vanilla pod and seeds, bring to the boil, add setting agent (as per instructions on the packet as they all vary in strength) and whisk well to combine.

Pour carefully into ramekins and place in the fridge to set – allow at least 4 hours.

Meanwhile, make a coulis by adding fruit to a pan and very gently warming through, adding a little water if required. Either mash or blitz in a food processor then pour through a sieve into a jug. Stir in maple syrup and a squeeze of lemon juice if required.

When the pannacottas are set, carefully turn out onto plates and pour the berry coulis around or over and garnish with a sprig of mint or more fruit. Enjoy the perfect wobble!

Notes

....

....

....

....

Mango surprise (serves 4)

This dish came out of trying to make tiny tartlets from nuts and, I think, coconut oil. The tartlets were frozen to set and then stuck in my tin, so I left them to defrost and of course they then crumbled to a mess so I placed them in the bottom of cocktail glasses and instead of filling tartlets, spooned the mango mousse on top of the nut mixture and served it to the guests. When asked what it was, 'Mango Surprise' came to mind. Surprised that the dessert looked rather lovely and that the guests enjoyed finding the 'surprise' as their spoons reached below the mango mousse. Any fruit can be used really.

12 walnuts
4 dates
½ tsp cinnamon
I large ripe mango, peeled, destoned and chopped
Juice of a lime
1 tsp fresh ginger or stem ginger

Blitz walnuts, dates and cinnamon together until a nicely textured mixture appears. Place in the bottom of a cocktail glass and press down slightly – not too much.

Wipe out processor bowl with kitchen roll, add mango, lime and ginger and process to a smooth puree. If fruit is too sharply sour, a spoonful of coconut cream (taken from a tin of coconut milk kept in the fridge to set the cream) gives a sweeter, smooth mousse. Pour onto nut mixture in glasses.

Top with toasted coconut flakes, crumbled toasted walnuts or a piece of mango.

Chia seeds can be added to the mousse for more fibre and nutrition and to provide a more set consistency.

Cakes, bars and biscuits

Ginger cake (serves 8 large or 12 medium slices)

This is one of our favourite post-yoga class healthy cakes. We serve a light breakfast over an hour before yoga so by mid-morning guests are ready for a nibble. Ayurveda doesn't encourage snacking so this should be eaten mindfully as a real treat – not every day!

175 g unsalted butter – melted (or 150 mL light olive oil)
100 g dried pitted dates
5 balls stem ginger
80 mL maple syrup
3 large eggs
200 g ground almonds
50 g rice flour
1 tsp baking powder
3 tsp ground ginger
1 pinch of salt (or none if you use salted butter)

Cover dates with boiling water and leave for 10 minutes, drain and food process with butter, maple syrup and stem ginger until mixed well.

Add eggs and blend.

Add all dry ingredients and blend.

Pour into prepared loaf tin or cake tin and bake at 170 °C for about 45 minutes or until skewer comes out clean. Try to allow to cool before eating!

Notes

....

....

....

....

Notes

....

....

....

....

Date and prune cake (serves 8 large or 12 medium slices)

Most of the guests have this one as their favourite. It is moist, spicy and light. We now usually make this gluten-free but we've given you vegan and gluten alternatives to try. It is ideal for vata, OK for pitta but a bit too heavy and sweet for kaphas – so just a small piece occasionally!

160 g pitted dates
90 g pitted prunes
300 mL water
1 tsp bicarbonate of soda
80 g butter at room temperature or 65 g olive oil or sunflower oil
75 g coconut sugar or other unrefined brown sugar
2 large eggs (or use flaxseed or chia 'eggs'*)
150 g spelt or wholemeal flour or gluten-free (we use 50 g rice flour, 50 g teff flour, 50 g fine polenta) or use yellow pea flour
1 tsp baking powder
1 tsp vanilla essence/extract
2 tsp mixed spice

Preheat oven to 160 °C, 325F or gas mark 3 or use Aga baking oven.

Place fruit and water in a saucepan and cook for 4–5 minutes until soft. Add the bicarbonate of soda and mash or blend. Beat together the butter (or oil) and sugar until light and creamy. Add eggs and beat to mix. Stir in the fruit mixture, then flour, vanilla, mixed spice and baking powder. Pour into cake tin, bake for 40–50 minutes until skewer comes out clean.

Can serve with cream (made with soaked cashews, lemon juice, water) with stem ginger pieces, or occasionally a decadent walnut sauce (60 g sugar, 120 g double cream, 2 tsp butter, handful of walnut pieces, pinch of salt) – melt sugar, add other ingredients, simmer until it's a light syrup.

*add 1 tbsp chia seeds or ground flaxseeds to 3 tbsp water and leave for 5 minutes

Damson or apple cake (serves 8 large or 12 medium slices)

This is a versatile mix to which you can add fruit such as whole stoned damsons, chopped apple and blackberries, mulberries etc.

150 g butter (or 135 mL light olive oil)
85 g unrefined caster sugar, or 60 g coconut sugar
3 large eggs
110 g spelt flour (for GF use rice flour 55 g, fine polenta 55 g)
75 g ground almonds
1 tsp baking powder
300–400 g damsons, apples or other fruit

Preheat oven to 160 °C, 325F or gas mark 3 or use Aga baking oven.

Using a hand mixer or food processor, cream butter and sugar until light and fluffy or, if using oil, until well incorporated. Add eggs one at a time beating after each one. In a separate bowl mix together the flour, baking powder and ground almonds and fold gently into cake mixture. Pour mixture into a prepared 20 cm diameter cake tin. Use a silicon spatula to clean the bowl and to roughly level mixture. Sprinkle on fruit which will sink during baking allowing the mixture to rise over and around it.

Bake for around 45 minutes or until skewer comes out clean.

Lovely served warm with a dollop of yoghurt or cream (dairy or oat or nut).

Notes

....

....

....

....

Vegan chocolate brownies (serves 9 large squares)

230 g very ripe banana (about 2 large bananas)
175 g flour (55 g rice flour, 60 g yellow pea flour, 60 g fine polenta)
2 tbsp organic cacao powder
95 g unrefined sugar
140 mL sunflower oil
140 mL water
1 tsp bicarbonate of soda
60 g Brazil nuts

Preheat oven to 180 °C, 350F or gas mark 4 or use Aga baking oven.

Mash banana in a mixing bowl or food processor. Add flour, sugar, oil and water, bicarbonate of soda and mix well. Stir in chopped Brazil nuts and pour into a prepared 20 cm square cake tin.

Bake for about 40 minutes or until a skewer comes out clean.

Notes

....

....

....

....

Apple flapjacks (serves approx. 10 slices)

This is a deliciously fruity flapjack, very different from the very sweet shop-bought type and a great way to use apples in the autumn time.

3 eating apples
400 mL apple juice from eating apples
1 tbsp cinnamon
1 large thumb of ginger
250 g jumbo oats
35 g sunflower seeds
150 g raisins

Heat oven to 180 °C

Leaving the peel on, chop apples and simmer with the juice until tender and all the juice is absorbed, purée in a food processor or with a hand blender.

Stir rest of ingredients into the apple puree and spread onto a silicon tray or lined baking dish.

Place in oven and bake for 30–40 minutes or until golden brown and firm. Score into slices and cool on a wire rack. Cut through into slices when cool enough.

Suggestions:

Replace some of the apples with prunes, fresh plums or damsons
Replace some of the raisins with a few dried cranberries
Stir in some chopped nuts

Notes

....

....

....

Plump-a-balls

These were designed for my Dad, who, at ninety-four, is a bit skinny now as his appetite isn't what it used to be. He has one or two of these balls with his afternoon cuppa and they are helping him gain a little weight. Full of good fats and nutrients from cacao and spirulina they help to get him up and working in the vegetable garden!

1 cup dates
½ cup almond butter
½ cup sunflower seeds
1 cup mixed nuts – cashew and Brazil
1 tbsp raw cacao powder
1 tsp spirulina
A little coconut oil if required to help stick mixture together

Blitz nuts and seeds in a food processor, then add the dates and process again, add all other ingredients and process until a sticky paste is obtained.

Roll into large balls – about size of a golf ball, roll in sesame seeds or desiccated coconut so they don't stick together, and look more beautiful. Or simply press mixture into a silicon tray and refrigerate. Cut into squares or bars. These will keep in the fridge for a couple of weeks (if you're lucky!) or they freeze well – always good to hide a few away as soon as they're made.

Notes

....

....

....

....

Pom bombs (makes 20 bombs)

We always serve a nibble after our morning yoga class. Although it's not great to snack often between meals, we serve a small breakfast a while before the yoga class so then afterwards guests are often a bit peckish. And after all, we want you to enjoy yourselves here and it gives us the chance to show you healthy cakes and nibbles – full of nutrients, no refined sugar and the minimum maple syrup or honey for sweetness, and often cinnamon or other spices to help with sweetness and digestion.

Since Mayan times thousands of years ago cacao has been known as Food of the Gods and now we know that raw cacao is a prebiotic – food for the good bugs in our microbiome, it is also a powerful antioxidant and supports production of feel good hormones. Several studies show that cacao flavanols can improve mood and cognition. Need a better reason? Combined with the astringent, antioxidant and vitamin-rich (C, E and K) nuggets of pomegranate seeds and we have Pom Bombs – they literally explode with flavour in your mouth, just try one.

50 g raw cacao butter
3 tbsp raw cacao powder
1 tbsp maple syrup
1 tbsp pomegranate molasses
1 pinch salt
1 pomegranate

Melt cacao butter slowly (I put in low oven of Aga) by placing in a bowl over, not touching, water simmering in a pan.

Meanwhile, carefully cut just the skin around the 'equator' of the pomegranate and pull apart. Gently ease out the seeds into a small bowl.

When the cacao butter has melted, quickly add the rest of the ingredients (except pomegranate) to it and combine well. Add pomegranate seeds and spoon a bite sized amount into small muffin cases or silicon mini muffin trays and place in the fridge to set.

Work quickly and don't heat the cacao butter too much or the chocolate will become grainy and dull.

Makes about twenty-four depending on the size of your pomegranate.

Notes

....

....

....

....

Bliss balls or modak

I first ate laddus at an Ayurveda retreat in Sri Lanka and then learned how to make them on a course there a few years later. Most use chickpea or wheat flour but then we made Modak one day and the doctor told us that the word means 'a preparation that makes the inner body happy' and that they were traditionally used to feed pilgrims. Such a lovely story that I felt inspired to have a go at making them. Rather than flour we used nuts and seeds one day, so I started with this idea. Here is our basic recipe, but after you've made these do feel free to add different spices and ingredients and enjoy!

They are great to have when you feel a little hungry, say at around 4 pm with a cup of tea. And infinitely more satisfying and healthier than a Hobnob!

1 cup raisins
1 cup dates
1 cup sunflower seeds
1 cup ground almonds
½ cup dried figs
½ cup goji berries
½ cup raw cacao nibs
½ cup ground flax seeds
1½ tsp spirulina
2 tsp coconut oil

Add a cup at a time to a food processor (otherwise a bit too much of a strain if everything added together). Make into balls and roll in desiccated coconut, cacao powder, sesame seeds, toasted chopped nuts so they don't stick together and to make them even more beautiful. Freeze or store in the fridge for a couple of weeks – if they last that long.

You can really try any flavours and ingredients you like; you just need to end up with something sticky enough to hold together. And if the idea of sitting mindfully rolling balls doesn't appeal, then simply press into a lined or silicon tray, score into bars or squares and refrigerate – easy!

More bliss ball suggestions:

Tahini, raw cacao powder, maple syrup, maca powder
Almond butter, tahini, dates, ground cardamom, cacao powder

Add fennel seeds to help digestion, cacao or matcha tea to give you a lift, maca to help balance hormones . . . let your imagination go wild!

Notes

Digest-a-balls

After learning from Anne McIntyre on one of her wonderful courses here that it's a good idea to finish dinner with digestive spices, digest-a-balls were born! These act as a signal to our digestive system that the fridge door is locked, and the kitchen door is closed for the day, no more nibbling!

So, I toasted the spices, took a teaspoon full and it was like chewing sawdust and such a strong flavour, I couldn't see myself doing that too often. So, I had the idea of making them more palatable. I toasted each type of spice individually so as not to burn them. Then ground them to a fine powder and added just enough raisins to enable small round balls to be formed – about the size of a large pea. This is all you need. Then, because the sweet taste is actually stimulating to our appetite, I mixed in coconut oil instead and that worked OK, but easier to press into a tray and place in the fridge and when cold cut into small, bite-sized squares. Have a go and see how you get on.

This mixture makes a good few weeks' worth!

½ cup fennel seeds
¼ cup coriander seeds
¼ cup sesame seeds
1 tbsp black cumin/kalonji seeds
1 tbsp cumin seeds
1 tbsp ajwain/carom seeds

Toast each type of seed separately and add to a processor for grinding. When you have a powder, add just enough raisins or dates or both to make the mixture stick together. Roll into balls then roll in sesame seeds to look lovely and prevent them from sticking together.

Chocolate beetroot cake (serves 8 large or 12 medium slices)

During the building work, every Friday I used to make the builders a cake and we'd gather round at 3 pm, review progress and discuss the plan for the next week. I'd only made about five cakes in my life before I moved here so the builders were my test audience. I'm afraid to say that although this was and is still one of my favourites, it was a vegetable too far for the builders. Unlike carrots or courgettes, grated beetroot is visible and colourful. It took me quite a few attempts to come up with this gluten-free version to which I've added chocolate which takes away some of the more obvious earthy beetroot notes. I hope you love it too.

Preheat oven to 160 °C, 325F or gas mark 3 or use the Aga baking oven.

2 large eggs (or 2 flax or 2 chia 'eggs')
Juice and zest of 1 large orange
1 tsp grated fresh ginger (I use a ginger grating dish to avoid bits of my fingers appearing in the guests' cake!)
1 tsp cinnamon
1 tsp allspice
¼ tsp freshly grated nutmeg
2 tbsp ghee – preferably melted
5 tbsp maple syrup
3 medium beetroot, grated
1 cup rice flour and ⅔ cup fine polenta (or 1⅔ cups yellow pea flour)
3 tbsp raw cacao powder
1 pinch of salt
2 tsp baking powder
½ cup raisins

In a mixing bowl beat eggs, then add all ingredients down to maple syrup and beat together. Stir in grated beetroot and then fold in the rest of the ingredients. Pour into a prepared 20 cm cake tin and bake for about 40 minutes or until a skewer comes out clean.

Teas

Teas are a great way to ensure our agni is robust which allows us to digest well, assimilate all the nutrients we need from the food we eat, produce the amazing tissues in our bodies and have some left over to top up our reserves of Ojas – the source of our vitality, immunity and zest for life!

Teas are good because they are warm, consist of herbs and spices to help digestion and are rehydrating. It is good to have a cup around 20–30 minutes before eating in order to rehydrate the stomach mucosa to ready it for pouring out acid and enzymes to digest the meal.

Note – only drink about a mugful with a meal, otherwise the digestive juices will be diluted too much. Often guests are used to drinking a lot of cold drinks with meals, this will definitely impair digestion! The body is an amazingly well-tuned machine operating at 37 °C so if too much cold water is added, the blood flow is directed to focus on keeping the vital organs at that perfect operating temperature and so redirects flow away from the digestive tract to those organs, which will impair digestion.

All culinary spices and herbs can be used to make teas so pick your favourite flavours and experiment!

The Clover Mill chai

We often serve this tea before the first night dinner as it sets the scene for an Ayurvedic dinner. It's the first thing we prepare, bringing it to the boil and then letting it infuse in the warm Aga oven for a couple of hours.

2 litres water
1 large cinnamon or cassia bark stick
20 green cardamom pods
5 cloves
5 black peppercorns

Crush the cardamom pods slightly with a pestle and mortar, add the pepper corns and give them a gentle tap, then tip into the water followed by the other ingredients. Bring to the boil and then gently simmer for at least 45 minutes. Strain and serve.

If you're not detoxing and therefore having caffeine you could add black tea and serve with or without milk.

Notes

....

....

....

....

Notes

Spice teas

Any spices can be used to make teas – just choose your favourites, mix and match and have a go! Generally, add a tsp to a litre of water, boil for 5minutes, strain and drink.

One of the best tridoshic teas to aid digestion, weight loss (I'm still drinking it…) and to balance all three doshas is CCF tea. Cumin, coriander and fennel.

Add a tsp of the seeds of each spice to a litre of water, boil, simmer for 5–10 minutes, strain and drink. Or strain into a flask and drink during the day.

We fill a large flask every morning so guests can drink it during the day.

Here are some of our favourites we serve at The Clover Mill:

Fresh mint – add a handful of fresh mint leaves to a large teapot and fill with boiling water, steep for 5 minutes and serve.
Fennel tea – just seeds and hot water
Cumin tea – just seeds and hot water
Coriander tea – just seeds and hot water
Black cardamom and coriander tea
Black Cardamom pods give a lovely smoky flavour and when added to coriander seeds the lemon flavour is enhanced.

Black Cardamom Tea

3–4 black cardamom pods
1 tbsp coriander seeds
1–2 star anise
1 tbsp fennel seeds
Add all ingredients to 2 litres water, bring to the boil and then simmer gently for 30–45 minutes, strain and serve.

The Clover Mill morning tea

Ginger is one of the most amazing spices, it's good for all doshas, great for stimulating digestive fire (agni), helping all stages of digestion and decreasing ama (toxins). Cinnamon adds sweetness and so makes this tea suitable for all doshas. Lime also stimulates agni and provides a refreshing way to start the day.

1 tbsp grated fresh ginger
1 tsp ground cinnamon or a squeeze of fresh lime

Grate ginger and place in a tea pot with a strainer (or use a cafetière). Add boiling water, steep for 5–15minutes, add cinnamon or lime and serve.

Or, if you want to prepare a large amount – add slices of ginger (with a stick of cinnamon) to a large pan of water and simmer for up to 30 minutes, strain and serve with lime.

Ginger tea with lime is the best drink to have first thing in the morning to wake up digestion. Or replace lime with lemon unless you are pitta in which case lime is better.

Fresh mint is also a lovely addition to ginger tea – or we use our ginger mint plant growing in the herb garden.

Notes

....

....

....

....

Cordials

Elderflower cordial

Cordials are a lovely way to bring nature indoors. I look forward to the elderflower blossoms to make elderflower cordial – always remember not to pick all of them otherwise you won't have any elderberries in autumn!

Although this is not a hot drink, do try to serve with at least room temperature water, and definitely no ice!

20–30 elderflower heads
2 litres water
1 kg sugar
2 unwaxed large lemons

First thing in the morning add water and sugar to a large pan and bring to the boil. Leave to cool slightly. Meanwhile, find a lovely basket, get your wellies on and go out to pick elderflower heads. They should break off easily.

Back in the kitchen after your lovely walk, add sliced lemons and elderflower heads to the pan, stir well and then cover pan and leave to infuse somewhere cool until the next day. Prepare sufficient sterilised bottles ready for the next day. Next morning, remove cover and smell the amazing elderflower cordial you have made. Pour cordial through a fine sieve or muslin into a large jug and then into the bottles. I keep some in the fridge and place a couple into the freezer.

To drink – dilute cordial with room temperature water and serve with a slice of lemon.

Notes

....

....

....

....

Elderberry cordial

A lovely autumn treat is to forage for berries and what a delight that we have many elder trees at The Clover Mill. Pick around 30 large heads dripping in purple berries.

30 elderberry heads
2 litres water
2 tbsp grated ginger
6 cloves
1 large cinnamon stick
½ cup raw honey (unheated and unfiltered local is best)

Use a fork to remove berries from the stalks. Add all ingredients to a large pan and bring to the boil. Simmer very gently for an hour without a lid so that the liquid reduces in volume.

Cool to room temperature before adding the honey. It is important to note that if honey is heated too much, in Ayurveda it's known to cause ama. Heating will reduce its amazing enzymes, vitamins and antioxidants. So, if you like it in your tea, wait until the tea is cool enough for you to drink before adding honey.

If you feel a cold coming on, then take a tsp of this mixture as often as you like, and it will reduce your symptoms.

Add warm water (not too hot!) to a few tsp of cordial for a lovely warming drink in the winter.

Notes

....

....

....

....

Milks

In Ayurveda the cow and her milk are revered. Of course, if you have your own cow in your back garden this is great, but for most of us, getting milk from our local supermarket is the norm. When you can, buy milk that hasn't been processed to death to last in the fridge for weeks. The pasteurisation process was a step-change in preservation allowing milk to be transported around at room temperature, but then the homogenisation to distribute the fat throughout the milk rather than let it sit on top (I used to love that bit when I was a child!) has, it seems, not been such a great idea. Our body isn't used to seeing such tiny fat particles and it's thought they might pass through a leaky gut to start an auto-immune cascade.

So raw is best, pasteurised but not homogenised is OK. Please note that although herds are frequently tested for pathogens such as TB and *Brucella*, I would only drink raw milk after heating.

Now there are many other milks on the market – from every nut and seed you can imagine, and more! And the good news is that they are pretty simple to make at home – cheaper and, more importantly, you know exactly what is in it! If you can use vibrant organic almonds to make your almond milk, even better.

Golden milk (serves 1)

It is impossible to walk down a central London street now without passing several coffee shops, all selling a huge variety of golden milks, turmeric lattes, matcha lattes, pumpkin lattes at Christmas – the list goes on!

In Ayurveda, remember this science is thousands of years old, golden milk was used to aid digestion, respiratory diseases, sleep, inflammation and many other uses.

Turmeric has bitter, astringent and pungent tastes and is heating making it suitable for all doshas. Its heating quality balances vata and kapha, its astringent and bitter tastes help mobilise kapha and its bitter taste balances pitta. Together with milk (dairy or nut) providing sweetness, golden milk pacifies vata, pitta and a small amount can mobilise kapha.

As with many herbs, black pepper massively enhances the absorption of the active components of turmeric into the bloodstream. So always add a grind of black pepper to a tsp of turmeric.

1 cup of milk (dairy, coconut, almond, hemp, or a mixture)
1 tsp turmeric powder or chopped fresh root
A little ground black pepper
¼ tsp fennel seeds
½ tsp cinnamon powder or cinnamon stick if boiling together
1 cardamom pod, crushed.

Add milk to a small pan and heat to almost boiling. Pour onto spices in a mug, stir and steep for 10 minutes before drinking.

Or, if making a large amount, add all ingredients to a large pan and bring almost to the boil, simmer for a few minutes and leave to steep for another ten minutes, then strain to serve.

Play around with the spices to find your own special flavour, bearing in mind your dosha too of course.

Suggestions:

Nutmeg
Star anise
Cloves
Grated ginger

Nut milk

1 handful of organic almonds
1 litre water

Place a handful of almonds in a bowl and cover with plenty of tap water and leave overnight.

In the morning, rinse nuts and place in a Vitamix or equivalent processor together with a litre of water. Blitz, allow to settle and then strain through muslin onto a clean jug or bottle. This removes the skins.

Other nuts or seeds to use are:

Cashews
Hazelnuts
Hemp seeds
Sunflower seeds
Pumpkin seeds

Notes

....

....

....

....

Matcha latte

We encourage most guests to reduce or remove coffee from their diet. After staying here is a good time as you will have gone through the worst phase of the caffeine-withdrawal headache and will be leaving feeling cleansed and energised. It's not the caffeine so much as the actual coffee that some Ayurvedic doctors believe is bad for us. I certainly feel much better for not drinking it daily. Coffee stimulates cortisol production when we're at rest and under stress and also affects our body's ability to process cortisol. Those of you who've attended our Rest & Digest Retreat know all about cortisol and how it affects our insulin levels and makes us crave sweet tastes causing weight gain, especially around the tummy and also impairs our immune response. So maybe that info will help you to reduce coffee intake!

I always think that if we're told we can't have something we want it even more, so I like to focus on what I'm adding to my diet rather than what I want to take out. The key is finding alternatives that you really want to have and for me, Matcha latte is a great coffee alternative as it satisfies the longing for a milky drink and helps if you're feeling tired or need to focus. I've had quite a few whilst writing this book! It can also be quite a ceremony, warming the milk, preparing the spices, adding a little warm milk to form a paste and then using a special Matcha whisk to combine the paste and warm milk. Sprinkle with freshly ground nutmeg, inhale and enjoy.

1 heaped tsp good quality matcha tea powder
½ tsp cinnamon
1 tsp freshly grated ginger
Pinch of freshly ground cardamom
1 cup of coconut, almond, oat or dairy milk
Sprinkle of freshly grated nutmeg

Add matcha tea powder, cinnamon, cardamom and ginger to a mug and add a little hot water to make a paste. Warm milk and pour onto paste, whisking continuously until well mixed. Sprinkle with a little nutmeg, sit down, inhale the aromas, and drink mindfully.

Hemp hot chocolate

This drink packs an enormous nutritious punch, combining three amazing foods – hemp milk, fabulous spirulina and raw cacao. Hemp seeds give us a complete protein meaning that they supply all nine essential amino acids that our body can't make. They are also a good source of protein, antioxidants, omega-3s, fibre, vitamins and minerals. Spirulina is another high-protein food made from dried photosynthetic bacteria and, weight for weight, is the most nutritious substance on the planet – you just can't have too much as it's a strong, 'acquired' taste! So, try to sneak it in drinks and sweets when you can. Cacao has been shown to reduce insulin levels, cholesterol too, reduces high blood pressure and improves metabolism. It acts as an antioxidant, is a prebiotic, and we all know the feel-good effects of a little raw cacao.

So, one day I decided to combine all three amazing products and it was surprisingly delicious! I don't have a sweet tooth anymore – I've trained my naughty sweet-loving bugs to hop off elsewhere – but you may need a small spoon of honey or maple syrup to enjoy this to the full.

Remember not to add honey until it's at drinkable temperature and that you can easily make your own hemp milk.

I cup of hemp milk – homemade preferably
2 tsp raw cacao powder
1 level tsp spirulina powder – or more if you can take it!

Make a paste in a mug with cacao and spirulina powder and a little hot water. Warm milk and pour into mug whisking until all the paste and milk is combined. Find a lovely seat outside, take a break and enjoy your nutritious drink.

Notes

....

....

....

Food cupboard essentials and nice-to-have

Fresh ingredients (seasonal fruit and vegetables)

Red onions
Ginger
Curry leaves* (can freeze)
Fresh coriander, mint, basil
Lemons and limes

Herbs and spices

Cumin seeds and powder
Coriander seeds and powder
Fennel
Cardamom
Fenugreek
Asafoetida
Turmeric
Ginger
Cinnamon
Black pepper
Black mustard seeds
Nutmeg*
Cloves
Smoked paprika*
Black cardamom*
Pippali*
Star anise*
Ajwain*
Black cumin (kalonji)
Liquorice*
Chilli
Mixed (sweet) spice
Garam Masala
Vanilla paste or essence or pods
Rose water*
Chamomile*
Oregano
Thyme

Nuts and seeds

Almonds – whole and ground
Cashews
Pumpkin seeds
Sunflower seeds
Chia seeds
Camelina seeds*
Black and white sesame seeds
Hemp seeds
Linseed/flaxseed
Tahini paste

Legumes

Mung beans
Split mung dahl

Grains and pseudograins

Rice – basmati and sona masoori
Oats
Quinoa
Red lentils

Flours

Spelt
Teff
Rice
Fine polenta
Green pea
Yellow pea
Quinoa
Buckwheat
Besan/chickpea
Coconut

Dried fruits and sweeteners

Dates
Prunes
Raisins
Figs*
Apricots
Goji berries*
Maple syrup
Coconut sugar*
Unrefined caster sugar
Raw honey
Raw cacao powder
Raw cacao butter*
Stem ginger

Refrigerated items

Unsalted butter
Fresh herbs and vegetables
Milks – almond, oat, dairy
Yoghurt

Oils and vinegars

Homemade ghee
Extra virgin olive oil
Coconut oil
Avocado oil*
Sesame oil*
Sunflower oil
Cider vinegar
Balsamic vinegar*

Miscellaneous

Desiccated coconut
Coconut flakes*
Baking powder
Bicarbonate of soda
Miso paste or fava bean paste
Tamari
Coconut aminos
Himalayan or sea salt
Baobab powder*
Lucuma powder*
Maca powder*
Tinned coconut milk
Kombu, seaweed flakes

* nice to have

Resources

Where to buy:

Spices – local Asian shops, or lovely organic ones can be obtained from www.steenbergs.co.uk

Pestle and mortar – I have the large 20 cm Jamie Oliver one and a few smaller ones acquired from trips to Asia.

UK-grown products such as the amazing gluten-free green and yellow pea flours, camelina seeds, quinoa, fava beans, etc. from https://hodmedods.co.uk

Bibliography and recommended reading

Inspiration for these recipes came from my time in Sri Lanka and India, and I'm an avid reader of recipe books, food blogs, food websites, and follower of food gurus, Ayurveda websites, etc. And these are just my top favourites:

Recipe books

Anand, Anjum. *Eat Right for Your Body Type*
Farrimond, Stuart. *The Science of Spice* (great for new tea ideas)
Hemsley, Jasmine. *East by West*
Lad, Vasant. *Ayurvedic Cooking for Self-Healing*
McVicar, Jekka. *Jekka's Herb Cookbook*
Tiwari, Maya. *Living Ahimsa Diet*
Yarema, T., Rhoda, D., Brannigan, J. *Eat, Taste, Heal*

Non-recipe book inspiration

Bunn, Mark. *Ancient Wisdom for Modern Health*
McIntyre, Anne and Boudin, Michelle. *Dispensing with Tradition*
McIntyre, Anne. *The Ayurveda Bible: Godsfield Bibles*
Pole, Sebastian. *A Pukka Life*
Pole, Sebastian. *Cleanse, Nurture, Restore with Herbal Tea*

Julie Dent runs The Clover Mill, an Ayurveda and yoga retreat in Herefordshire that became fully booked soon after opening in 2013. Whilst searching for a suitable chef, Julie took on the role and developed delicious ayurvedic meals that the guests love. Using mainly home grown and foraged, fresh and seasonal vegetables and fruits, The Clover Mill menus were established. Repeated requests for recipes and then a book, resulted in *Cooking with The Clover Mill*, Julie's first recipe book.

In here you will find most of the recipes served on the retreats.